Cloister and Community

Mary Jo Weaver

Cloister and Community

Life within a Carmelite Monastery

Indiana University Press
Bloomington and Indianapolis

HOUSTON PUBLIC LIBRARY
R01245 93290

This book is a publication of
Indiana University Press
601 North Morton Street
Bloomington, Indiana 47404-3797 USA

http://iupress.indiana.edu

Telephone orders 800/842-6796
Fax orders 812/855-7931
Orders by e-mail iuporder@indiana.edu

© 2002 by Mary Jo Weaver
All rights reserved

No part of this book may be reproduced or utilized in any form or by any means, electronic or mechanical, including photocopying and recording, or by any information storage and retrieval system, without permission in writing from the publisher. The Association of American University Presses' Resolution on Permissions constitutes the only exception to this prohibition.

The paper used in this publication meets the minimum requirements of American National Standard for Information Sciences—Permanence of Paper for Printed Library Materials, ANSI Z39.48-1984.

Manufactured in the United States of America

Library of Congress Cataloging-in-Publication Data

Weaver, Mary Jo.
Cloister and community : life within a Carmelite monastery / Mary Jo Weaver.
p. cm.
Includes bibliographical references.
ISBN 0-253-34184-1 (alk. paper)
1. Carmelites of Indianapolis—History. 2. Carmelite Nuns—History.
3. Teresa, of Avila, Saint, 1515-1582. I. Title.
BX4324.I53 W43 2002
271'.971077252—dc21
2002003326

1 2 3 4 5 07 06 05 04 03 02

FRONT COVER: SOUTH CORRIDOR, LOWER LEVEL, C. 1941

FRONTISPIECE: FRONT ENTRYWAY, C. 1963

PAGES ii/iii PHOTOGRAPH: ARCHITECT'S DRAWING OF PROPOSED MONASTERY

PAGES iv/v PHOTOGRAPH: MIRROR IMAGE OF MONASTERY FROM OUTSIDE ENCLOSURE WALL, WINTER 1955

for my sisters,

Kathryn, Margaret, and Thérèse

Contents

I am grateful to the members of the Carmelite community in Indianapolis, who have been generous in the extreme, allowing me not only access to the archives, but also rare opportunities to share their lives as much as that is possible for an outsider. My ability to write their story almost from inside their space gives it a character it would have lacked had they not opened the house and themselves to me for the past few years. What began as a relatively modest archival document has, thanks to them, turned into something much more complex and interesting.

All of the sisters have contributed to the production of this book and to the well-being of its author, but I must single out some of them for special thanks. Mary Rogers, my architectural tour guide, suffered a stroke and died as the book was being finished, which makes my eternal gratitude ever more real. She entered the monastery in 1939, and thanks to her memory, I am now able to find the seams of new construction and to know what rooms looked like many years ago. Thanks to her determined ingenuity, we know the first name of the mysterious Mr. Marchetti, who did much of the stonework in the cloister. Betty Meluch, by sometimes making chapters part of her spiritual reading time, examined them with care and good will and offered me many helpful suggestions. There are things in this book that would not have been there had it not been for the kind help of Rachel Salute. Helen Wang found photographs for me and took ones I needed. My dear friend Jean Alice McGoff supported this idea from its inception, was an invaluable guide to the archives, stayed cheerful as I pressed her into reading chapters over and over again, and helped with innumerable little details. One of the best parts of my life over the last twenty years or so has been my friendship with these sisters.

SISTER MARY ROGERS, 2001

I owe thanks as well to those who helped me with bibliographic suggestions and clearer expressions of Carmelite history. Kate Myers, Keith J. Egan, and Dyan Elliott knew the best books and the sharpest angles of interpretation as I tried to make my way through a great deal of contextual material. My copy editor, Jane Lyle, did her usual excellent work and helped to make things consistent. I am grateful to those friends who read this work and offered suggestions, particularly to Luke Johnson and Joanne Wolski Conn, whose knowledge of religious life from inside and outside makes them particularly good critics. My colleagues in the Department of Religious Studies at Indiana University are a steady source of support and delight to me.

I am always touched by the power of novelists to portray the life of a religious community. Rumer Godden's *In This House of Brede* (1969) takes readers into a large, cloistered Benedictine community in England before the second Vatican council. Mark Salzman's *Lying Awake* (2000) invites us into a contemporary Carmelite monastery in California where sisters dress and behave much like nuns in earlier centuries. Each writer stands outside community life, but has an insider's sympathy. I tried to find that balance as I wrote this history. Like an outsider, I know the myths of Carmelite life, and so sometimes dream of myself in the great mystical adventure buoyed up by the community and hidden in solitude. Like an insider, I know some of the shadows as well, and see that overly busy schedules and the minor irritations of daily life are not absent from the cloister. Beneath all these perspectives—fictional and real—is the challenge to find a community of intimacy that draws one deeper into self-knowledge and, one hopes, closer to a compassionate life.

I participate in a variegated community of love and understanding through the generosity of many friends: the Carmelite sisters in Indianapolis, especially Jean Alice; old friends in faraway places like Gena DiLabio; my sister Thérèse and her family; David Brakke and Bert Harrill; Julie Bloom along with her parents, Fran and Bud, and her husband, Richard Balaban; and my faithful friend of so many years, Susan Gubar, and her partner, Donald Gray. To all of them, my thanks for years of kindness and, recently, for listening to me think through and work through this book.

Cloister and Community

W

S N

E

FLOOR PLAN OF THE COMPLETED CARMELITE MONASTERY

FIRST BUILDING: 1930-33

FIRST ADDITION: 1936-37

SECOND ADDITION: 1940-41

THIRD ADDITION:1960-61

Introduction: A Tapestry

This story of the Carmelite monastery in Indianapolis began as a short architectural history, marking the changes that occurred in the physical structure from the first wing (1932) to the installation of the new doors between choir and chapel (1988). Yet, as I studied plans, read through archival material, and walked through the corridors, I realized how dynamic this building has been and continues to be. The monastery has changed to accommodate the needs of the sisters, who, in turn, have responded to the exigencies of the times. A proper history of the monastery, therefore, needs to include the story of the people who have lived in it, and to explore the events that shaped their lives. Furthermore, the population of any Carmelite monastery is of course the sisters who make up its particular community, but it also includes the shaping ideas of Carmelite life. Specifically, I believed that I had to tell the story of Saint Teresa of Avila and her reform movement along with some general Carmelite history in order to place the Indianapolis Carmel into context. I wanted to chart the dramatic changes in the lives of a group of sisters who left the world to participate in a late medieval life but are now deeply committed to the world through their Web site, www.praythenews.com. My challenge, therefore, has been to weave these various threads together into a kind of tapestry, one that adds detail and color as it moves from the early years of the twentieth century into the new millennium.

While writing the book, I have often reminded myself of the Bayeux tapestry, which was created to celebrate the Norman Conquest of England at the Battle of Hastings (1066). Although technically not a tapestry, this embroidered work was created in eight pieces and then sewn together to form a piece of cloth approximately 230 feet long and nearly 2 feet wide, displaying eight different colors. Legend attributes this marvelous feat to Queen Matilda, wife of William the Conqueror, but a more likely explanation attributes it to an embroidery school somewhere in England, perhaps in Canterbury. Whatever its origins, it is a beautiful, complex, highly detailed work that pleases the viewer. I have tried to do the same here, using several themes and colors to weave the fabric of this monastery into a coherent story.

I have divided the book into six chapters corresponding to the way the monastery was constructed. It was built or modified in six stages: the concrete foundation (1930), the east wing (1932), a small extension to the south (1936), the completion of the monastic cells (1941), the building of the permanent chapel (1960), and the addition of the new doors between the choir and the chapel (1988). The drawing shows the stages of development, and photographs (historical and contemporary) illustrate the building plan and the life of the community. I have tried to keep the story flowing smoothly by putting some of the information in notes at the end of each chapter. I found, for example, that too much detail about certain rooms and how they had changed clogged the narrative and threatened to overtake the project. At the same time, I did not want simply to discard those aspects of the architectural history.

Chapter 1, "Creating Sacred Space," introduces the basic concepts of sacred space and early Carmelite history, as well as Saint Teresa of Avila's experience of religious life and her ideas for reform. It ends with the "foundation" of the Indianapolis monastery, meaning the work of its founder, Emma Seelbach (Sister Theresa of the Trinity), the early years in New Albany, the transfer of the monastery to Indianapolis, and the actual pouring of the concrete foundation of the building, events covering the years from 1922 to 1932. This chapter, therefore, establishes the groundwork and the pattern that will be embellished in subsequent chapters.

Although Teresa entered a large, bustling monastery in Avila, she was determined to base her reform on three principles: her monasteries were to be small, unendowed, and enclosed. The next three chapters are designed to explore those aspects. Chapter 2, "A Few Rooms/A Few Sisters," is about size or smallness and covers the years from 1932 to 1936. It starts with the small beginnings of Teresa of Avila's reform movement in mid-sixteenth-century Spain, the movement to which this monastery is related. It gives a brief description of the geography of the reform from Spain to America. The architectural feature of this chapter is the first (east) wing of the monastery. We will take an imaginative tour of the building as it was in 1932, when one wing had to house living quarters, work space, meeting rooms, a public chapel, and the choir.[1] The chapter ends by anticipating the death of Mother Theresa Seelbach and reminds us of the small beginnings of the Indianapolis community.

Chapter 3, "Content with Little," is about poverty, its place in the Christian tradition and in monastic life. I describe Teresa's experience as a privileged young woman eventually drawn to found an unendowed monastery, and then discuss poverty and detachment in the Indianapolis community as it took shape from 1936 to 1941. The building project in this section is a small addition to the south wing, the entry of additional sisters into the community, and the landscaping project that produced the "cliff" in front of the building. It ends with the inauguration of the annual novena to Our Lady of Mount Carmel, an event that drew thousands of participants from 1939 to 1974.

Chapter 4, "Never Out/Never Seen," is about enclosure and silence as the twin protections for a life of solitude. It explains the history of enclosure in general, and how Teresa's experience in an unenclosed convent led her to insist on strict enclosure in her reform movement. Architecturally, this chapter focuses on the completion of the living quarters and other events from 1941 to 1960. Although the sisters at that time wanted to build a grand church on the north end of the building, the influx of vocations meant that they really needed more cells and a more accommodating kitchen. In this building phase the permanent walls enclosing the yard around the monastery were finished.[2] The chapter ends with accounts of two foundations or daughter houses, one in Terre Haute (1947) and another in Reno, Nevada (1954), and looks ahead to how things were beginning to change a little bit behind the enclosure wall.

Chapter 5, "Moving Stillness," considers prayer and mystical union in Christian history and in Teresa's experience, and describes the building of the permanent chapel in 1960-61. Since it encompasses the years immediately following the second Vatican council, it focuses on the Indianapolis community as a visionary group, open to the exploration of new territories. Changes in the church opened a new theology of contemplative life, including a dynamic concept of cloister, to which the sisters responded. This openness to new ideas is a reflection of Teresa's own struggles to come to terms with a new form of prayer in a particularly dangerous time and place. The building of the chapel also coincided with changes in the income-producing work of the community, as the sisters began a typesetting business that would eventually lead them to produce an inclusive-language Psalter and other books, such as *The Woman's Prayer Companion* and *God in Ordinary Time*. In the meantime, the sisters were exploring new forms of prayer and monastic silence and beginning to invite people into their new choir to celebrate liturgy with them.

Chapter 6, "A Door to the Universe," examines spirituality, specifically a new spiritual consciousness rooted in tradition and given new form by the second Vatican council and contemporary theological reflection. It begins with an outline of Christian spirituality, paying particular attention to the insights of Pierre Teilhard de Chardin. His work and that of creation-centered spiritual thinkers and cosmologists have shaped some of the thinking that led the sisters to establish a Web site in order to share their spirituality with the world. I envision an imaginative Easter vigil scene to bring many of these ideas together. The architectural feature of this chapter is the installation of the new doors between the choir and the chapel, created to evoke life as an evolutionary resurrection.

If the book has a plot, it is this one: The community that began in 1932 as a group living in a sacred space apart from the world has changed over time into a community that sees the world itself as a sacred space. Teresa of Avila believed that God dwelt at the deepest center of one's soul, desiring to be found through contemplative prayer in community. Translated into the language of the new creation story, God dwells in and longs to be discovered in the heart of the universe. Those who enter the monastery still seek silence and cloister, but in a more dynamic form through which one turns toward the world to gather its pain and its joy and then turns inward to explore the deep mystery embedded there. In the process of opening toward the world and withdrawing to their inner silence, the sisters explore the cosmic dimensions of contemplation.

Notes

1 Cloistered communities are separated from the public in all things, including worship. The language of that separation is evident in the distinction between the chapel (where the public attended worship) and the choir (where the sisters met for prayer and liturgy). The means of separation were usually doors and grilles, latticed walls that were often covered by a curtain so that the sisters could not see or be seen when attending Mass.

2 The monastery was built on an 18-acre piece of property, and the building itself contains 10,000 square feet of space. The permanent walls surrounding the monastery enclose 5 acres, one of which is the monastery itself.

1 Creating Sacred Space

This chapter sets the foundation for the concept of sacred space, and for an understanding of Carmelite history. I describe two different kinds of sacred space before I situate the Carmelite order within its early history. Then, in order to lay the foundation on which the book will be constructed, I introduce Teresa of Avila's intention to create monasteries that were small, enclosed, and without endowments, concepts that will be discussed more fully in chapters 2 through 4. With the groundwork covered, I introduce Emma Seelbach, whose vocation to Carmel eventually led to the establishment of the monastery in Indianapolis (1932) by way of New Albany, Indiana. Finally, we get a look at the concrete foundation of the Indianapolis Carmel, which was poured in 1930.

TWO HOLY PLACES

Furnace Mountain Monastery, a Buddhist temple and retreat center south of Lexington, Kentucky, was built on an existing sacred space. To Buddhist eyes, the particular isolated valley in which the temple stands is hallowed ground, a natural nesting place for the Golden Phoenix, whose egg is a symbol for transformation. From the highest peak of the 350-acre site, looking down on the temple, one can see two mountain ranges. According to the ancient Chinese principle of feng shui,[1] the "Blue Dragon" (a yin symbol) on the left and the "White Tiger" (a yang symbol) on the right meet in a valley that contains a "Golden Phoenix," a knoll with a creek in front of it. The temple is built precisely there, between yin and yang, facing the Golden Phoenix. Those who come here to pray sit confidently in a natural sacred space, connected through time to the very essence of Being.

Sacred space can also be created. When the fourth-century Christian emperor Constantine moved the imperial capital from Rome to Byzantium, he did so for political reasons. Constantinople, the magnificent city he built for himself, was meant to be a monument to his ambition and his new religion, designed to outshine ancient Rome in every respect—even its holiness. Rome's reputation as a holy city for Christians derived in part from its association with martyrdom: those who met ghastly deaths in the Roman Colosseum were said to be special bearers of God's glory. How else could they witness for the faith with such calm heroism? Their bones, hidden away and revered by a persecuted Christian community, were scraps of the sacred, reminders of God's presence within this group. Rome's particular distinction rested with the bones of two martyr-saints, Peter and Paul, the great leaders of the early Christian movement.

OPPOSITE: EMMA SEELBACH, C. 1911
PREVIOUS SPREAD: COMMUNITY AT RECREATION IN THE COURT, C. 1951

Constantinople had nothing that could compete with the relics of Rome until Helena, Constantine's sainted mother, made a pilgrimage to Jerusalem and there found the cross on which Jesus had been crucified and the nails that had held him there. When they were brought to Constantinople, magnificent churches were built for them, songs written to celebrate them, ceremonies created to install them. A century later, when the empress Pulcheria returned from Jerusalem with relics of Mary—an icon said to have been painted by Saint Luke, her shroud, and her cincture—she, too, built great churches to display and honor them.[2] Invested with these supremely holy objects, Constantinople became a sacred place. Those who prayed in its churches stood on ground made holy by the presence of Christianity's most sacred relics.

TWO THEORIES

Whether sacred space exists on its own or is created to fill a religious need, it is invested with meaning; it grounds believers in a tradition, locates a spiritual center, and provides a place where one can be closer to the divine, or touch it in some way.

If scholars agree that sacred space is important to religious groups, they disagree about what it is. One school of thought, following the lead of Mircea Eliade, argues for the presence of naturally sacred spaces on earth: holy hills and fountains, mountains whose majesty embodies divine power are scattered across the earth waiting to be discovered. Eliade and those who share his views tend to divide the world into two components—one primitive, the other modern—and to privilege the ability of pre-literate peoples to "see" the sacred spaces in the world. In this way of thinking, modern people cannot find the holy places that exist in their midst; we do not know how to associate space with cosmogony.[3] Yet twentieth-century Buddhist monks found a naturally occurring sacred space in the hills of Kentucky.

Another group of scholars, represented by Jonathan Smith, argues that human beings manufacture sacred space.[4] One can see an active intellectual process at work to "put things in place" and mark the boundaries of power. The creation of sacred space orders society by establishing and controlling centers of spiritual power. The resplendent church Hagia Sophia, the supreme achievement of Byzantine architecture undertaken by Constantine's successors, is an example of a sacred space created to celebrate the power and piety of the Christian Empire. Its ornate ritual celebrations reinforced the perception that this monumental basilica was sacred space.

CREATED SACRED SPACE

Although Christians claim some natural holy places—Jerusalem and some of the mountains of Israel, for example—most Christian sacred space has been created. To be sure, there are stories about holy wells or sacred groves in Western Christianity, but for the most part holy places are connected with churches, monasteries, and shrines, built to house or display the sacred. Churches nourish the devotional life of believers through the ceremonies of their tradition; sacred rituals are performed there, sacraments celebrated to mark the momentous events of their lives. Sometimes a church takes on an added aura of holiness because of a dramatic event—pilgrims streamed to Canterbury Cathedral in the Middle Ages because Thomas à Becket had been martyred there—but the sacred space of churches is generally more ordinary. Monasteries and convents are essentially communities of women or men who have taken vows of poverty, chastity, and obedience in order to live a common life and dedicate themselves to prayer. Created as sanctuaries for those seeking a way to God, they were usually built in remote places so that nuns and monks could separate themselves from the distractions of the profane world. In some medieval and modern European usage, women live in monasteries and men in convents. The American custom is typically the reverse, though contemplative orders of nuns usually refer to their dwelling places as monasteries. Shrines are often associated with extraordinary events or sacred objects: they are created around stories of embodied holiness, appearances of Mary, or relics of saints that effect cures or bring comfort. As such, they usually attract pilgrims because of their reputation for curing illness or answering prayers. The most magnificent examples of created sacred space are the great cathedrals of medieval Europe. Their size alone—huge towers, cavernous interiors, enormous stained-glass windows—command attention and respect, even as they invite people inside. Their dark interiors, aglow with flickering candles and decorated with familiar statues, were places of sacramental exchange where holy things—water, pictures, music, anointing, forgiveness, and communion—were available to those who entered. Explaining that space creates awareness, architect Yi-fu Tuan says that the medieval cathedral deepened a person's sense of the divine. In an ordinary setting, God, heaven, and the saints are only words, and the imagination is limited, "but in the cathedral [the] imagination need not soar unaided . . . the beauty of space and light . . . enables [one] to apprehend effortlessly another and far greater glory."[5]

SOME CARMELITE HISTORY

The Carmelite monastery of Indianapolis is neither a holy locale like Furnace Mountain nor a great cathedral like those that marked the landscape of medieval Christendom, but it has connections to both kinds of sacred space. The sisters trace their origins to Mount Carmel, the site of Elijah's dramatic victory over the priests of Ba'al (1 Kings 18.1-46). The connection with Elijah draws our attention to other holy places in his story: Mount Horeb (Sinai), site of God's covenant with Israel, where God was revealed to Elijah in "a sound of sheer silence" (1 Kings 19.12), and the "wadi at Cherith," where God commanded ravens to feed him (1 Kings 17.3). Carmelites, therefore, have an imaginative link to dramatic holy places in the landscape of ancient Israel.

The historical origins of this religious order began around 1200 C.E., when a few pious laymen from the Latin Kingdom of Jerusalem were drawn to take up the adventure of an isolated ascetic life. Their attraction to solitary, contemplative spirituality was nurtured by a general renaissance of eremitical life in the eleventh and twelfth centuries.[6] When monasticism, which had begun in the desert experience of early Christian hermits, became a complex, organized system in Europe, reformers looked for new ways to follow Christ into the desert. Monasticism, they said, was best understood as flight from the world, an imitation of Christ that entailed poverty and asceticism. These early Carmelites were laymen—perhaps they had gone on crusades to the Holy Land—who saw themselves as successors to Elijah, drawn to a hermit's life and a prophetic vocation. Their formula of life, written by Albert, patriarch of Jerusalem, between 1206 and 1214, was brief, Scriptural, and non-legalistic, fostering the call to solitude and continual prayer.

When Carmelites began to move to Europe, c. 1238, they had to reinvent themselves. Even their clothing was a problem. Their official habit included a brown and white striped cloak, inspired, they said, by Elijah. If their clothing was appropriate in the Middle East, it was ill-advised in Europe, where striped clothing was considered satanic. When Carmelites were ridiculed and even assaulted because of their "devilish" garb, Pope Alexander IV ordered them to stop wearing the cloak. When they refused, they set off a protracted set of negotiations involving several popes. By the time Pope Boniface VIII issued a bull banning striped clothing from all religious orders in 1295, the Carmelites had adopted a white cloak.[7]

We should remember that Europe in those days was a dynamic, changing world: an agrarian way of life was giving way to an urban one; university education, new occupations, and a rising middle-class population all created challenges for the church. Carmelites, engaged in solitary prayer in rural settings, did not fit: they had no ecclesiastical status and no apostolate. Compared to Dominicans and Franciscans, orders created by charismatic founders with a clear sense of purpose in this new world, Carmelites looked irrelevant. Compared to Benedictines and Cistercians, who had huge holdings of land and deeply rooted histories, Carmelites had no place. Whereas the diocesan clergy had rights to say Mass, preach, and hear confessions, Carmelites did not have the same privileges. They seemed to have no real founder, and it was not clear that they had a right to exist in a church that was continually judging the legitimacy of new religious orders.[8]

Into this distressing situation came someone who led the Carmelites into the mendicant way of life. Although there is no indication that this person was Saint Simon Stock (d. 1265), a story began to circulate in the early fourteenth century that Stock was an

TERESA OF AVILA. PAINTED BY FRAY JUAN DE LA MISERIA, O.C.D., 1576

Englishman whose life of solitary prayer eventually led him to start a Carmelite foundation in England.[9] The murky historical records of the time make it impossible to say more, but we do know that a general chapter (community meeting) held at Aylesford, England, sent two men to Pope Innocent IV to approve adaptations to the way of living. In 1247, therefore, their formula of life, now a Rule, was promulgated. It allowed Carmelites to locate in urban settings, to live together in houses (rather than in "desert places"), to shorten their time of strict silence, and to modify their laws of fasting and abstinence to a certain degree. These changes made it possible to be a Carmelite in thirteenth-century Europe: very quickly, the Carmelites moved into cities (especially university towns), took advantage of educational opportunities, and were granted ordinary clerical privileges. They were now called friars—they called themselves Brothers of Mary of Mount Carmel—and participated in the church's work in Europe. Their apostolate usually involved preaching and works of mercy rather than schools and hospitals. They claimed and defended Elijah as their founder and maintained their identity as men with vocations to solitary prayer.[10]

Ironically, just as they began to flourish in Europe, the church entered one of its worst historical periods, one marked by schism, abuses of power, general laxity of religious life, plague, and war. Carmelites, neither better nor worse than other groups, were caught up in this unfortunate situation. Holy, reforming leaders worked hard but could not dispel "the general mood of decadence within the Order." Chapter records of the time show us that there were constant admonitions to return to Carmelite discipline and observance, to no avail. As events throughout Europe and in the church grew worse, it looked as if the friars would not reform. In this context, those attending the chapter (large general meeting) of Nantes in 1430 accommodated the Rule to current behavior. According to Peter-Thomas Rohrbach, a not unbiased source, this now "mitigated Rule of 1430 struck a lethal blow at the very essence of Carmelite life; it was a radical departure from the prophetic vocation."[11]

According to its critics, the mitigated Rule destroyed the Carmelite spirit of prayer and solitude. They saw the heart of the rule in paragraph 7: "Let each one remain in his cell, or near it, meditating day and night on the law of the Lord and keeping vigil in prayer unless occupied with other lawful duties."[12] The mitigated Rule freed them to walk around and converse, behaviors that led to a number of reform movements in various places that hoped to return the Carmelites to the original Rule. Since they were only marginally or temporarily successful, the mitigated Rule of 1430 defined Carmelite life until the sixteenth century, when an unschooled and unusual Carmelite nun in Spain did what no one else had been able to do: she returned herself and others—at first a few in Spain, and eventually many all over Europe—to the primitive Rule, to a life of solitary prayer and prophetic witness.

TERESA OF AVILA AND A NEW SENSE OF SPACE

Spanish Carmelite life was reformed and renewed by Teresa of Avila (1515-82) and John of the Cross (1542-91), both saints and doctors of the church. Teresa founded her new monasteries on the primitive Rule (actually the one approved by Innocent IV in 1247), and so infused them with a new spirit of adventure built upon solitude and community. She also gave her sisters a new architectural sensibility: her monasteries were small and cloistered.

In one reading of church law, all nuns from the fourteenth century onward were to be "perpetually enclosed," to live in houses where no one came in and no one went out.[13] Cloistered monasteries were sometimes built in isolated settings; if in a more populous place, they were often constructed on a courtyard model, where rooms opened onto interior space and put their backs to the world outside. In this architectural space one could enjoy some of the benefits of being outdoors while still being closed off from the distractions of the world. In fact, however, enclosure was not the only model of religious life for women in the sixteenth century. In Teresa's Spain, some religious women lived in cloistered houses and recited the Divine Office at specified times of the day and night; others lived together piously with neither enclosure nor the obligation to say the Office; still others lived in monasteries where they recited the Office, but were not cloistered.[14]

La Encarnación, the monastery Teresa entered in 1535, was of this last type: it was a courtyard structure, but as large and busy as a modern hotel. The sisters said the Office but did not observe enclosure. There were class divisions within the house, where nuns from poor families lived in dormitories, while their wealthier counterparts occupied apartments with servants and family members.[15] Be that as it may, life at the Incarnation was often austere and was always dependent upon the patronage of wealthy families. Because the sisters needed this kind of support and relied on it to provide food, clothing, and medical care for themselves, they were continually called upon to visit with noble ladies and gentlemen, to pray for them, placate them, and sometimes travel to their estates to be entertained and entertaining.

Teresa's reform, begun in the 1560s, included three points that were extrapolated into the architecture of her houses: monasteries were not to be obligated to rich patrons; they were to have no more than thirteen sisters; and they were to maintain strict enclosure. She envisioned Carmelite monasteries as small, simple, contained spaces built around a central courtyard with grounds surrounded by a wall. Visitors were to be rare events rather than a daily distraction as they had been in unreformed convents, and the independent status of the monastery was meant to free the sisters for lives of quiet work and contemplative prayer. Silence, recollection, and the struggle for inner transformation were to replace chatter, repetitious devotions, and the need to please others.

ORIGINAL VISION OF THE INDIANAPOLIS CARMEL

Before ground was broken for the Carmelite monastery in Indianapolis, a vision of it existed in the mind of its founder, a member of the Carmelite community in Bettendorf, Iowa. Emma Seelbach (1881-1936), the daughter of a prominent Kentucky family, was studying opera in Europe when she read the autobiography of Saint Thérèse of Lisieux and felt herself drawn to Carmel. Because this beautiful, musically gifted thirty-year-old woman discovered cloistered Carmelite life in Europe and was unaware of its existence in the United States, she decided to enter a monastery in England. We can imagine, therefore, that her vocation was shaped in a setting that still had its feet in the medieval world, where monasteries were sometimes attached to impressive churches and were centers of a spiritual universe for those who lived nearby.

MOTHER THERESA SEELBACH, C. 1925

Her desire to become an English Carmelite, however, was not to be fulfilled. Instead, when she had to return home for her father's funeral, she discovered an American Carmelite tradition and chose to enter the monastery in Davenport (later Bettendorf, and still later Eldridge), Iowa, in 1912. She became Sister Theresa of the Trinity in 1913, and made her final profession in 1914. All the energy she had directed toward the study of music was now aimed at spiritual transformation, and she entered into the life with pas-

ORIGINAL MONASTERY IN NEW ALBANY, INDIANA

sion and determination. Carmel, she said, was the first thing in her life that had completely absorbed her.

When Bettendorf decided to make a foundation, to open a daughter house in another part of the country, the prioress chose Sister Theresa, hoping that her intelligence, talent, and family connections might enable her to found a monastery in Louisville, Kentucky. For a number of reasons, however, the new foundation was finally located in the diocese of Indianapolis, and in 1922 three sisters moved into a small frame house in New Albany, Indiana, that had been converted into a temporary monastery. Emil Zurschmied, the young man who transformed this old house into a monastic space, later became the caretaker of the monastery in Indianapolis, retiring in 1957.

After a shaky start, with some young women entering and then leaving the group, the young community in New Albany began to take hold. As it outgrew its small, temporary structure, Sister Theresa made plans to build a permanent monastery in Indianapolis. When we look at those original plans, we can see a vision of Carmel that was shaped in the European tradition: the monastery was consciously designed to look like the city of Avila, with its parapets and towers. It had a medieval personality with its castle-like turrets, a high, surrounding stone wall, and a grand monastic church. In the economic boom of the 1920s, such plans seemed eminently reasonable. Promises of financial help from a generous benefactor, the steady vision of a gifted architect, and the dedicated energy of Mother Theresa conspired to create a picture of an ethereal Carmelite monastery.

The architects, Jacob Edwin Kopf and John Deery, designed a building of 10,048 square feet to sit nearly 300 feet from the road on an 18-acre tract of land a half-mile north of 16th Street on Cold Spring Road. It would stand across the street from the VA hospital and Coffin Golf Course, and was supposed to have a landscaped park in front of its walls. The land was ideally suited to the plans, but when the stock market crashed in October 1929, those grand dreams had to be revised, at least for the time being.

THE FIRST PLAN AND THE TUNNEL

Once it was clear that there were not sufficient funds to complete the project, the sisters had to decide how to proceed. Their instinct was to build the first floor of the entire monastery. In 1929, therefore, workmen dug the foundation for the entire building, including an infirmary wing that was never built. In August 1930 they poured a concrete floor over what were then called cellars, unfinished underground spaces with dirt floors that housed utility pipes, electrical wiring, furnaces, coal bins, and other necessities.

The monastery's underground space—which the sisters call "the tunnel"—is unusually pleasant, well lighted, meticulously marked, and spacious. Although today one can walk upright in it (taking some care to duck under pipes), it was not always quite so lofty. According to local tradition, a friend of the sisters used WPA workers to dig out the tunnel in the 1930s. In the 1950s, when Americans were building fallout shelters in their back yards, the sisters did not need to do that. They simply cut a hole in the bottom corner wall of the Novitiate Room and put a ladder down into the tunnel, which was equipped with a stove and adequate shelter.

WORKING ON THE FOUNDATION, C. 1930

Once the foundation had been poured, workmen began to build the outside walls. Before they finished—in fact, they had completed part of the east (front) wing and only a small part of the south one—Mother Theresa and Mr. Kopf made a different decision. They were concerned that building only the first floor all the way around would leave them with a structure that looked more like a bunker than a monastery. The architects revised the blueprints and the construction plan to complete both floors of the east wing. Since this part of the building is what people see when they come through the front drive, it made sense to present its best face to the world.

THE MONASTERY AS SACRED SPACE

The ground on which the monastery stands is not hallowed, except in the sense that the whole created order bears a divine imprint. There is no holy fountain here, no relics, no shrines to extraordinary heavenly visitations. The grounds themselves are not particularly auspicious: they are rather ordinary acres in a Midwestern urban setting. Although the monastery was designed to house a shrine to Saint Thérèse of Lisieux, the "Little Flower," it was not built on a mountaintop or nestled into some glen of extraordinary beauty. Yet, what might take one's breath away is the consistency of life in this setting: it has supported a community of women dedicated to prayer for almost seventy-five years.

The monastery fits the model of a created holy place, one with specific ideas about the boundaries between the secular and the sacred. After the monastic tradition of the Catholic Church developed a concept of sacred space as something apart from the world, those who entered monasteries or convents "left the world" to find holiness in an enclosed space sealed off from the outside. As that tradition has developed in the modern world, some groups continue to maintain strict enclosure and to find meaning in the demarcation between their sacred space and the outside world. In the Carmelite community of Indianapolis, there has been a long and prayerful journey to a different sense, to a perception that the world itself is a sacred space.

Notes

1 Feng shui, a 4,000-year-old tradition, is the art of arranging space, particularly one's home or workplace, to enhance health and happiness. Its underlying principle is harmony with the energy (chi) of one's environment.

2 See Kenneth Holum, *Theodisian Empresses: Women and Imperial Dominion in Late Antiquity* (Berkeley: University of California Press, 1992), pp. 142-47, 226.

3 See Mircea Eliade, *The Quest: History and Meaning of Religion* (Chicago: University of Chicago Press, 1967), and also his *The Myth of Eternal Return: Or, Cosmos and History* (Princeton, N.J.: Princeton University Press, 1954). See also Paul Wheatley, *The Pivot of the Four Quarters: A Preliminary Enquiry into the Origins and Character of the Ancient Chinese City* (Chicago: Aldine Publishing Company, 1971).

4 Jonathan Z. Smith, *To Take Place: Toward Theory in Ritual* (Chicago: University of Chicago Press, 1987).

5 *Space and Place: The Perspective of Experience* (Minneapolis: University of Minnesota Press, 1989), p. 116.

6 For a reading of early Carmelite history, see Joachim Smet, O.Carm, *The Carmelites: A History of the Brothers of Our Lady of Mount Carmel*, vol. I, *Ca. 1200 A.D. until the Council of Trent*, chapter 1 (Private printing, 1975; rev. ed. 1988). Another discussion of Carmelite origins is Wilfrid McGreal, *At the Fountain of Elijah: The Carmelite Tradition* (Maryknoll, N.Y.: Orbis Books, 1999).

7 Michel Pastoureau, *The Devil's Cloth: A History of Stripes and Striped Fabric* (New York: Columbia University Press, 2001). Pastoureau, an expert in medieval heraldry and the history of Western symbolism at the École pratique des hautes études in Paris, discovered abundant documentation from the twelfth and thirteenth centuries emphasizing the diabolical quality of striped clothing. As he pursued his interest, his main case study became that of the Carmelites moving into Europe with their striped cloaks in the thirteenth century.

8 The Fourth Lateran Council (1215) decreed that there could be no more "new" religious orders, and that if new orders were founded, they had to adopt one of the already existing and approved "Rules." Since the Carmelite Rule had been written between 1206 and 1214, Carmelites argued that they were, indeed, founded before Lateran IV; but since no papal approval had been granted before 1214, others argued that they were not legitimate. Pope Honorius III intervened in this dispute to confirm the Carmelite Rule (January 1226), an act that was confirmed by Gregory IX (in 1229).

9 Simon's importance is affirmed by Rohrbach (see note 10), but not by Smet (see note 6), which, since Smet is a more reliable historian, argues for a shadowy role for Stock. Carmelite historians also debate the nature of the mitigation and its interpretation. Keith J. Egan says that the legends of Elijah, Mary, and Simon Stock need to be analyzed, not simply jettisoned. See his insightful article "The Spirituality of the Carmelites," in Jill Raitt et al., eds., *Christian Spirituality: High Middle Ages and Reformation* (New York: Crossroad, 1987), pp. 50-62.

10 Peter-Thomas Rohrbach, *Journey to Carith: The Story of the Carmelite Order* (New York: Doubleday, 1966), explains the Elijah connection this way: Carmelites in need of a founder (to compete with Dominic and Francis) chose Elijah because he was an archetype for them. Elijah had a solitary life and a prophetic vocation; he was prayerful, God-possessed, and brave. That Carmelites looked back for inspiration to Elijah and Elisha is actually asserted as early as the 1281 Constitutions, which Rohrbach was not aware of (I thank Keith J. Egan for this information). The Constitutions of 1324 claim that Carmelites stand in an unbroken line of prophetic hermits on Mount Carmel from Elijah to the present, a claim bereft of historical evidence. When a Dominican challenged the Carmelite John Hornby to debate the issue at Cambridge in 1374, John won the argument and also secured the claim: members of the university could no longer question it. As late as 1725, Pope Benedict XIII allowed Carmelites to erect a statue of Elijah in Saint Peter's, identifying him as the "founder of the Carmelites." I found a curious footnote to the Elijah story in the *Indianapolis Star* (1932) explaining the proposed monastery: "founders trace its history to the establishment of the kingdom of Israel by Elijah, his wife supposedly instituting an order of women recluses." I cannot determine where Mrs. Elijah came from.

11 Rohrbach, p. 111, explains that though the actual changes were concerned only with fasting, abstinence, and solitude, contemporary Carmelites realized what the mitigation implied. "These reductions in solitude and austerity were a major divorcement from Carmel's historical traditions, practices which profoundly changed the inner spirit of the Order and its original vision. The prophetic vocation, the imitation of the prophet Elijah, demanded solitude and an intensive program of penance, and with an abandonment of this tradition the Order was beginning a further confused descent."

12 Michael Mulhall, O.Carm, ed., *Albert's Way: The First North American Congress on the Carmelite Rule* (Barrington, Ill.: The Province of the Most Pure Heart of Mary, 1989), p. 7. This book contains, among other things, the texts of Albert (1206-14) and Innocent IV (1247) in Latin and English along with a variety of interpretations and studies.

13 Women religious, unlike their male counterparts, were not permitted to work in the world until the seventeenth century. On the contrary, as Pope Boniface VIII put it in his papal decree *Periculoso* (1298), "nuns collectively, and individually, present and in the future, of whatsoever community or order, in whatever part of the world they may be, ought henceforth to remain perpetually cloistered in their monasteries." For the Latin text of this decree, along with a thorough reading of commentaries on it, see Elizabeth Makowski, *Canon Law and Cloistered Women: Periculoso and Its Commentators, 1298-1545* (Washington, D.C.: Catholic University of America Press, 1997); quotation from p. 135.

14 See the Introduction to *The Collected Works of St. Teresa of Avila*, 2nd ed., vol. 1, translated by Kieran Kavanaugh and Otilio Rodriguez (Washington, D.C.: ICS Publications, 1987), pp. 18-21.

15 See Jodi Bilinkoff, *The Avila of Saint Teresa: Religious Reform in a Sixteenth-Century City* (Ithaca: Cornell University Press, 1989), chapter 5.

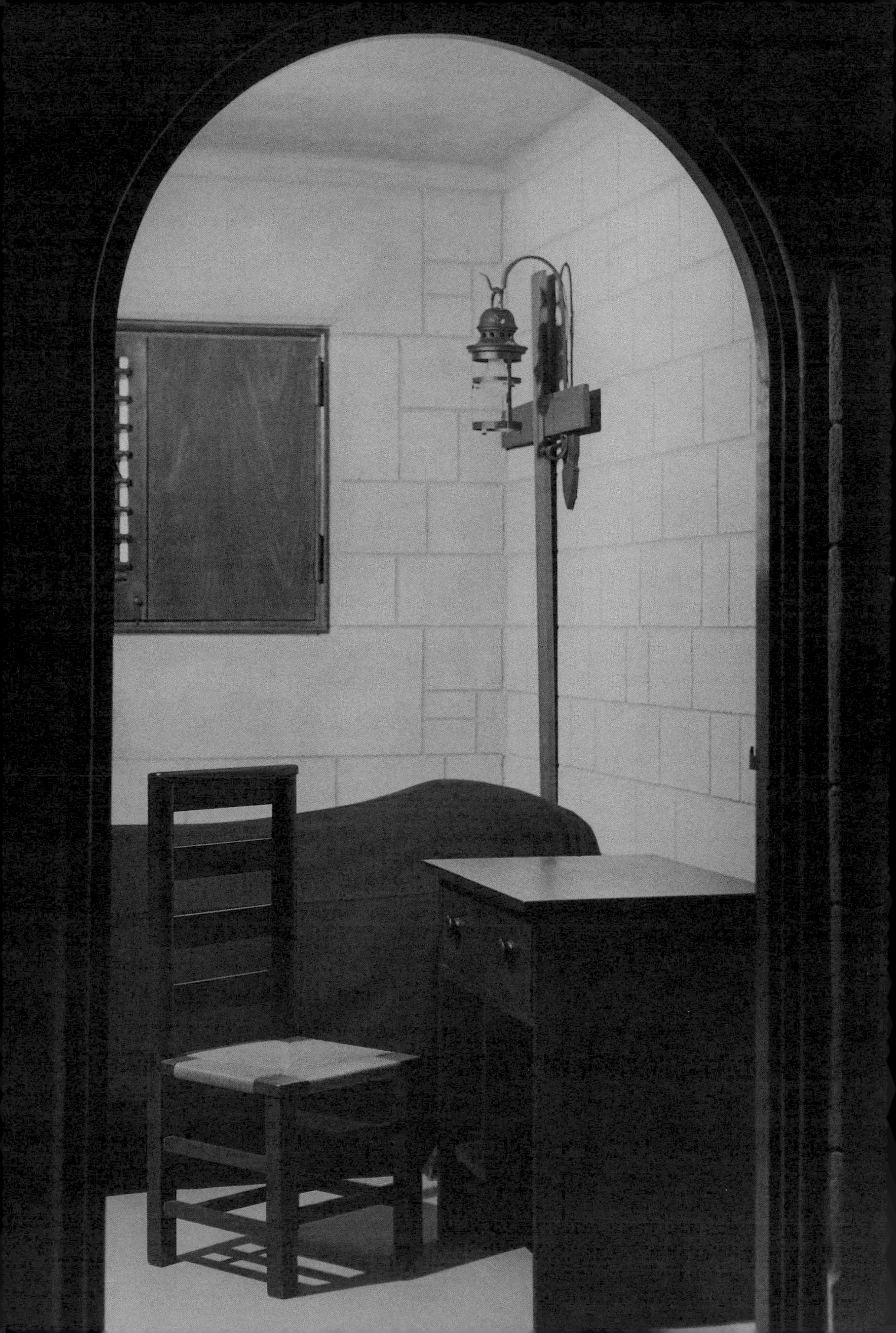

2 A Few Rooms/A Few Sisters

This chapter is about size, the modest beginnings of Teresa of Avila's reform movement and her insistence that monasteries be "small in every way." I then describe the small group of five sisters who began monastic life in Indianapolis in 1932 and note events in their lives up to 1936, when the next building project began. The historical section focuses on the admission of women to the Carmelite order in the fifteenth century. We then look at the construction of the first wing of the Indianapolis Carmel and a report of the public tour of the building before the sisters were literally locked in to begin their life in this new monastery.

"SMALL IN EVERY WAY"

In August 1562, on the feast of Saint Bartholomew, four young sisters received the Carmelite habit at Saint Joseph's, the small, rugged monastery that was the first of Teresa's reformed houses. For a variety of reasons, the foundation was made clandestinely.[1] When she looked at what she had accomplished, Teresa, still a sister in the monastery of the Incarnation, was riddled with devilish doubts about whether she had done the right thing, and even whether she herself had the courage to "shut [herself] up in so austere a house" (*Life* 36.8). A visit to the Blessed Sacrament settled her heart and shored up her courage. Although Teresa adapted her ideas about actual size to allow an increase from thirteen to twenty sisters, her idea that a monastery should be small was never in doubt. She may have been influenced by the Jesuit idea that the company should be small, select, virtuous, and detached, but she was also working against the enormous size and administrative headache of the monastery of the Incarnation.

In Teresa's day, Carmelite convents were independent from one another and reflected great diversity of intention and practice. Some were small and cloistered, while others permitted nuns to have contact with people; some were dedicated to solitary prayer, while others supported a rather non-demanding life. Carmelite convents in Spain were originally *beatarios*, communities of *beatas* (devout women living and praying together who often retained their own money, had suites of rooms, and received visitors freely). In 1479, a wealthy widow, Doña Elvira Gonzalez de Medina, founded a *beatario* in her house in Avila with two other women. Dedicating it to Saint Mary of the Incarnation, she limited it to fourteen women in honor of Christ, the Blessed Virgin, and the twelve apostles, all following the Carmelite Rule (in its mitigated form). In 1495, the Catholic monarchs gave her a site for a new convent, which opened officially in 1515.

OPPOSITE: TYPICAL CELL (SISTER'S ROOM), C. 1940
PREVIOUS SPREAD: COMMUNITY IN COURTYARD, 1934

During the next twenty years, *la Encarnación* grew enormously, housing more than one hundred nuns when Teresa entered it in 1535.[2] The nuns recited the Divine Office[3] and performed other religious exercises (such as saying prayers for their patrons), but they were neither a small group nor an enclosed one. Nuns received a steady stream of visitors, went out freely, and entertained guests in their rooms. As God led Teresa through the reform of her own life over the next twenty-seven years, she learned to value austerity and solitude. Accordingly, she dreamed of a small, quiet, enclosed house where she could live with those detached from worldly vanity, to converse about God and find comfort in solitude. When she founded Saint Joseph's, her model was Christ, "who had no house but a stable." Monasteries, she told her sisters, "must be poor and small in every way" (*Way* 3.9).

SMALL BEGINNINGS IN INDIANAPOLIS

On a sunny October day in 1932, the feast of Saint Thérèse of Lisieux, Joseph Chartrand (1870-1933), the fifth bishop of Indianapolis, celebrated Mass at the newly finished Carmelite monastery. Intoning the solemn rites of the church, he consecrated the "Carmel of the Resurrection" and then locked the small community in behind a polished enclosure door. These five sisters—Mother Theresa Seelbach and Sister Hilda Ammann from the monastery in Iowa, and three young women who had entered at New Albany—were now "dead to the world," dedicated to solitary prayer and community life.[4] In the mental universe of 1930s Catholicism, the monastery constituted a "powerhouse of prayer." In the history of the diocese, it was a dream come true.

FIRST WING OF MONASTERY, C. 1938

MOTHER THERESA SEELBACH'S GRAVE

Carmel had had a special place in the heart of Indianapolis even before its existence as a diocese. Simon Bruté (1779-1839), the first bishop of Vincennes (later to become the diocese of Indianapolis), was a special friend to the sisters in the Baltimore Carmel. He met them during his years in that city and wrote to them often from Indiana. His letters frequently asked for their prayers and expressed his determination to have a Carmelite monastery in his diocese.[5] The fifth bishop of Vincennes, Francis Chatard (1834-1918), was the first bishop to reside in Indianapolis.[6] As a member of an old Baltimore family, he also knew and loved Carmel all his life. Although he was in his eighties and quite ill when he was approached by the Bettendorf Carmel about founding a monastery in his diocese, he instructed his coadjutor and successor, Joseph Chartrand, to extend a warm welcome to the sisters. Just shy of one hundred years after Simon Bruté expressed his fervent desire for a Carmelite monastery in his diocese, therefore, the sixth bishop in his line of succession consecrated the Indianapolis monastery.

The beginnings of the Carmel of the Resurrection, though not as vexed as those of Saint Joseph's in sixteenth-century Avila, were nevertheless rather difficult. The community did not grow in numbers in the early years, and there were some serious structural concerns, including persistent leaks in the roof. In these years of the Depression, there were also financial worries. Whatever the burdens, Mother Theresa carried them in silence and was determined to lead her small community into a gloriously envisioned future. In November 1935, however, Mother Theresa suffered a serious heart attack, and the sisters were told that she would not survive another one. She did not. When a second attack struck on May 25, 1936, she faded in and out of consciousness until she died on June 11th, the feast of Corpus Christi. The new bishop, Joseph Ritter (1892-1967), described her as a "woman of unusual character, gifts, and qualifications . . . [with] a magnetic personality and a strong character."[7]

When she was buried in the small enclosure that eventually became the monastery courtyard, the future was first in the hands of Mother Hilda, and then, after her nervous breakdown in 1937, in the hands of the young sisters who had come with Mother Theresa from New Albany. By early January 1938, Sisters Miriam (age 31), Agnes (age 29), and Anne (age 32) constituted the Carmelite community in Indianapolis. Their difficulties would not have worried Saint Teresa: in her work of creating new foundations, she had encountered hostile townspeople, recalcitrant ecclesiastical officials, leaky roofs, tumbledown houses, imperious noblewomen with tendencies to denounce her to the Inquisition, physical ailments, and lice. It seemed to her that the "Lord desired that no foundation be made without some trial in one way or another" (*Foundations* 24.15).

Had Teresa of Avila looked down from heaven upon these three young sisters, she might have given them the same advice she continually gave to her own sisters: "If you have confidence in Him and have courageous spirits—for His majesty is very fond of these—you need not fear that He will fail you in anything" (*Foundations* 27.12). Apparently, these women were imbued with just those virtues. The new addition to the south wing (which will be described in chapter 3) was in progress when Mother Theresa died. In the meantime, the life of prayer and work in an atmosphere of austerity and love went on as surely as the monastery began to take fuller shape.

WOMEN IN THE CARMELITE ORDER

As religious life grew and flourished in Europe during the Middle Ages, most religious orders of brothers provided for a corresponding sisterhood. Some, however, did not think that women could adequately pursue their particular vocation. Cistercians, for example, were not eager to welcome women into their ranks, though they eventually accepted them.[8] Carmelite friars, faced with their own challenges in late medieval Europe, did not accept women members until the middle of the fifteenth century, partly because they did not want to assume fiscal and supervisory responsibility for them. As Carmelite friars fell into the general decline that affected the entire church in the fourteenth and fifteenth centuries, however, Blessed John Soreth, Master General of the Carmelite Order from 1451 to 1471, thought that women might be the very ones to strengthen and confirm the mystical character of the order. Accordingly, he petitioned the pope for permission to establish an order of Carmelite women.

The papal bull *Cum Nulla*, published by Nicholas V in 1452, granted Carmelites permission to establish a "Second Order" of women.[9] Soreth, a reformer within the order, was eager to accept women who would lead secluded, prayerful lives embodying the "better part" chosen by Mary of Bethany in the Gospels (Luke 10.42). In early May 1452, therefore, he accepted some Beguines into the Carmelite order. Typically, Beguines aspired neither to marriage nor to the convent, but lived together in households where they prayed together, read and discussed religious books, did a variety of apostolic works, and supported themselves by begging and with their needlework.[10] Their unattached status was unacceptable to church officials, however, and when they were ordered to adopt an existing religious Rule in the mid-fifteenth century, some of them chose the Carmelite one. The women accepted by Soreth had been under Carmelite spiritual direction and wore a Carmelite habit. From this small group, Carmelite sisters spread to northern Europe, France, Italy, and Spain.

Since the sisters were founded in the mid-fifteenth century, they followed the Mitigated Rule of 1430. Soreth instructed his new sisters to admire God's works in nature, read Scripture, and lead lives of introspection. They were to observe the Rule, to sing choral Office according to the Carmelite tradition, to renounce all possessions, and to observe enclosure.[11] Although Soreth's vision of Carmelite sisterhood was one of an enclosed community leading lives of solitary prayer, his reforming energies did not reach Spain, a relatively isolated section of Europe. In addition, attempts to regulate religious life on the Iberian Peninsula had to pass muster with the Catholic monarchs, Ferdinand and Isabella, whose own reforming instincts led them to be suspicious of directives from outside the country. Religious reform in Spain, therefore, came from within the country with support from the crown, which explains why Teresa of Avila sought the endorsement of King Philip II during her own attempts to reconstitute Carmelite life in the sixteenth century.

The complexities of church/state relations throughout Europe, and the challenges faced by religion in general in the early modern period, meant that the founding of Carmelite monasteries there was seldom simple or easy. When Anne of Jesus and Anne of Saint Bartholomew took Teresa's reforms to France, for example, they had to negotiate with the crown and with ecclesiastical officials whose ideas differed from theirs. Like all religious houses in late-eighteenth-century France, Carmelites were caught in the Revolution. Francis Poulenc's opera *Les Dialogues de Carmelites*, first performed at La Scala in 1951, celebrates the courage of a group of Carmelite nuns who were guillotined during the French Revolution.[12]

American Carmelite history was not so dramatic. Separation of church and state ensured that Carmelites in this country could pursue their dreams without government interference. The family tree of the Carmelite monastery of Indianapolis traces back to Bettendorf (Eldridge), Iowa, a daughter house of the first Carmelite monastery in the United States, the one founded at Port Tobacco (now the Baltimore Carmel) in 1790.

THE FIRST WING OF THE INDIANAPOLIS MONASTERY

The revised plan for the monastery called for contractors to complete both floors of the east wing, part of the south wing, and the boiler room. Although this first section of the monastery was small, it had to contain everything the sisters needed to maintain themselves and to begin their lives as a prayerful presence in the city. Accordingly, this first section of the monastery contained cells (bedrooms) for each sister and workrooms set aside for the making of vestments and altar breads, along with normal household rooms (dining

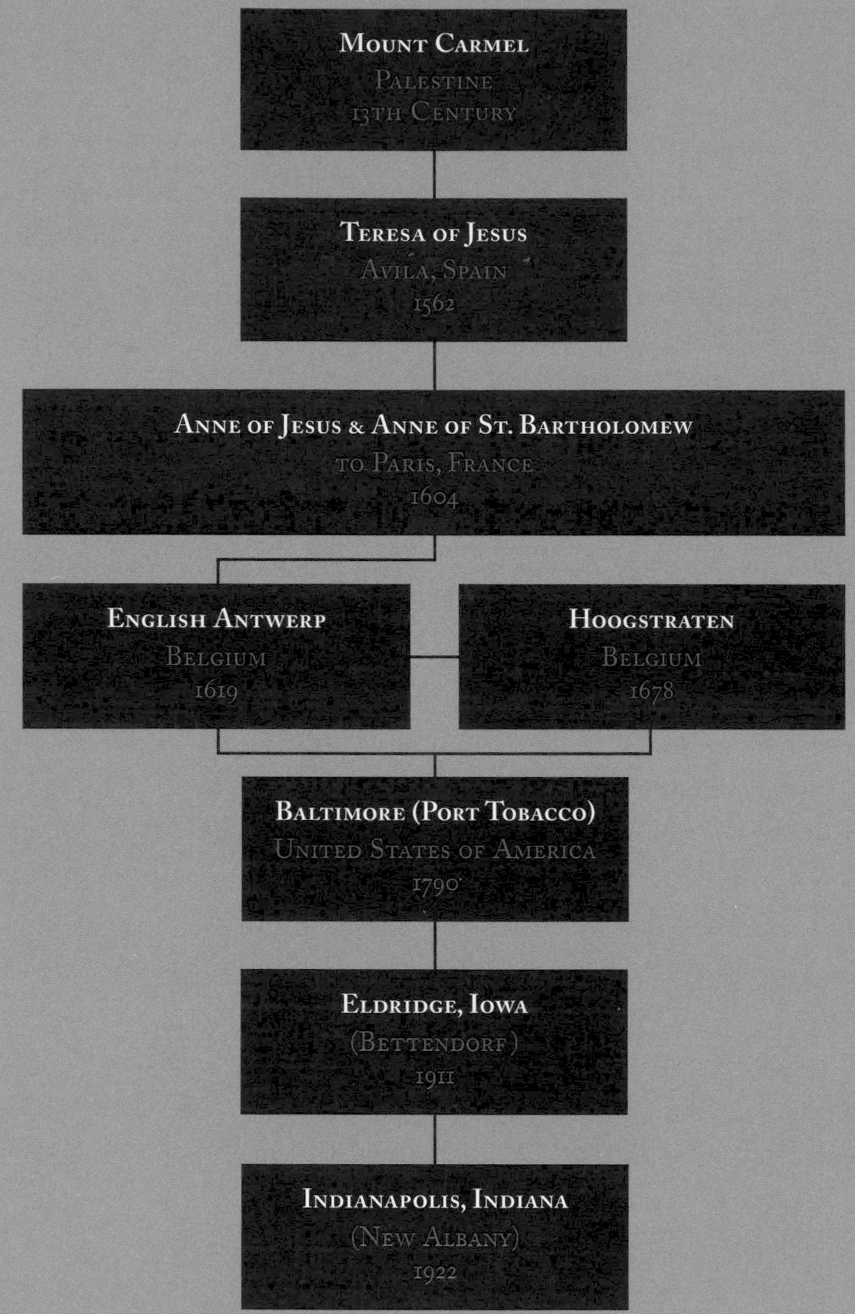

CARMEL OF THE RESURRECTION FAMILY TREE / INDIANAPOLIS, INDIANA

room, kitchen, laundry, closets, bathrooms). Because of the nature of community life and the need to assemble together, it had different kinds of meeting rooms. All sisters met in the Assembly Room; those sisters who held administrative offices met in the Council Room; and those sisters in the early stages of the Carmelite vocation met in the Novitiate Room. In addition, this small first section of the monastery contained a library, some offices (including one where sisters could see a doctor or dentist), and a "turn room" where sisters could communicate with people through a small, curtained door.

The heart of the monastery was the choir. Dreams of a large church to be built on the north side of the monastery were still alive in these early years; it would be grand, divided into a side for the faithful and a cloistered side for the sisters. The temporary chapel in the first wing contained the essentials in miniature. It was divided by a grille (a latticework wall behind which the sisters attended Mass), and the cloistered side had some benches along each side. This is where the sisters prayed several hours each day—saying the Divine Office at appointed hours and making two hours of quiet, personal prayer—kneeling or sitting back on their heels on the floor.

The parts of the monastery that would have been open to the public in the early years have been changed to suit new purposes. Stewart Brand says that buildings "learn" and "behave," that they have a life in time intimately connected to those who live in them.[13] That has surely been true of the monastery: it has adapted itself several times since its beginning, its structures sometimes reflecting new stages of consciousness within its community.

We can take an imaginative tour of the public parts of the early monastery by approaching it from three directions. From above, we get a sense of how the first piece fits into the larger plan. The turrets on the southeast corner are dramatic and functional,[14] anchoring the two sides of the building. Only a few rooms were built on the south side (workrooms, cells, and some meeting rooms), and the next building phase would extend that section to include six more cells and two bathrooms. The main part of this original structure was the east wing, which was built up to, but not including, the north side towers.

From the outside, we can see some of the ideas that inspired Mother Theresa as she planned her ideal monastery. A headline in *The Indiana Catholic* in September 1932 gave a verbal picture: "Behind Castellated Walls of Stone Nuns of Carmelite Order Will Retreat from World," it said, and described a "fortress of prayer" built of rough stone with turrets, parapets, deep, small-paned windows, and a castle-like entrance. According to the story, the architects designed the building from personal observations of old monasteries and castles in Europe. Mother Theresa wanted the monastery to evoke Avila, a city in old Castile, seventy miles northwest of Madrid, surrounded by massive granite walls from which rise eighty-six towers. Suitably awed by the towers, we might next notice the front entrance: the large front door with hand-wrought iron fittings is set within a six-foot recess

LEFT: CARMELITE SEAL; RIGHT: STATUE OF HOLY MOTHER TERESA IN FRONT WALL

surrounded by arched stonework containing the shield of Carmel with its various symbols surrounded by its motto.[15] The quotation—*zelo zelatus sum pro domino deo exercituum*—is from the Vulgate (the Latin Bible), 3 Kings 19.10. The Douay Bible used by most Catholics in 1932 translates it this way: "with zeal have I been zealous for the Lord God of Hosts."[16] In a recessed niche on the front wall, there is a statue of Teresa of Avila (*Sancta Mater Teresia*), which is nearly six feet tall and displays two famous aspects of the saint. It shows her power as a writer (she is holding a book and a writing implement) and her experience as a mystic (an angel beside her holds the arrow of God's love).[17]

From inside the front door we can wander back through time to those early years when the monastery had two shrines to the Little Flower. Just inside the front entrance, in an alcove to the left, was a replica of the body of Thérèse of Lisieux propped up at an angle in a glass coffin. She was dressed for burial, in a Carmelite habit, crowned with roses, holding a crucifix on her breast in her right hand and a rose at her side in her left hand. This popular saint, who was so important in the vocation of Mother Theresa Seelbach, was seen in the Indianapolis Carmel in one of her most dramatic iconic presentations.[18]

SHRINE OF THE LITTLE FLOWER

At the top of the stairs in its own niche is a statue of Mary, Queen and Beauty of Carmel ("*Regina decor Carmeli*"), a Marian title used by Carmelites. Someone standing in front of the statue could turn left and walk past the enclosure door into a small hallway leading to the temporary chapel.[19] Turning right, one would not have been able to walk into or even see a corresponding hallway on the other side. It was originally designed for "extern sisters,"[20] but since the three young sisters who moved into the monastery from New Albany lived and worked in those rooms, they were part of the enclosure.[21]

To the right of the statue of Mary was the "turn room." In a cloistered monastery, the "turn" is an enclosed roundtable that can be rotated to receive gifts or mail; the "turn room" also contains a small door where it is possible to talk to one of the sisters through a curtained grille. Someone who did not wish to ring the turn bell could proceed straight through a doorway[22] into a shrine of Saint Thérèse that was behind a grille because that space also served as a temporary visiting room for sisters and their guests. There a statue of the Little Flower stood on a small pedestal, and visitors to the shrine could kneel there and pray. The rest of the east wing was cloistered: no one from "the world" could come in (save for doctors and dentists when necessary), and no one from the enclosure could go out. A visitor in the 1930s could only imagine the other parts of the house and respect them as sacred spaces available to a small group of consecrated women whose lives were dedicated to prayer and penance in a remote part of an urban setting.

PUBLIC INTEREST

In 1932, when the first phase of the building was finished, the sisters opened the entire monastery to visitors. Once the sisters were enclosed there, no more visitors would be permitted to enter most of the house, so this was a rare opportunity for people in the Indianapolis area to walk through the halls and rooms of this unusual building. Before its opening to the public, there was a private tour for the governor, Harry G. Leslie, accompanied by the president of Indiana University, William Lowe Bryan, and the president of the Indiana Board of Agriculture, O. L. Reddish. On Friday, September 2, nuns and priests were invited to see the monastery, and on Saturday and Sunday it was open to the interested public from 10 A.M. until 6 P.M. Although there was a steady downpour on Saturday, crowds began to gather at 7:30 in the morning. By the time the doors opened, 5,000 were in line; 50,000 visitors came through over that two-day period, and 5,000 had to be turned away. The electricity had not yet been hooked up, so visitation was restricted to daylight hours. Because of the overwhelming interest the place held for the public—only half of them from Indianapolis—it was opened again the following weekend to another 50,000 visitors.

The Sunday rotogravure (photograph) section of the *Indianapolis Star* on October 2 provided a sepia-toned tour in pictures for those who had not been able to walk through the house. The photographer captured the curved interior corridors fashioned in stone or cement, the iron grillework, the cells, the great oak doors studded with iron nail heads, the hand-wrought hardware, the shrines and niches. The photographs evoke a medieval atmosphere where pale light filters through small stained-glass windows, where the very halls are resplendently quiet, waiting for the sisters whose lives would begin in that new space the next day.

NEW LIFE TAKES SHAPE

The few sisters who began Carmelite life in Indianapolis were guided by the Rule and Constitutions revised and developed by Teresa during her reform movement in sixteenth-century Spain. It is not clear, however, to what degree Teresa studied the Carmelite Rule when she entered the monastery of the Incarnation. It formed the juridical basis of her life, but in those early years it did not form her. When we read her life, we see that her desire for personal prayer was awakened not by the Rule, but by reading non-Carmelite books.

The Third Spiritual Alphabet by Francisco de Osuna, a Franciscan spiritual writer, helped her to begin a practice of interior prayer. *The Confessions of Augustine* led to her "conversion" experience when she was thirty-eight years old. Her journey toward union with God, directed by God and shaped by years of solitary prayer and reflection, ultimately led to a reform movement and to the Rule and Constitutions followed by the sisters in Indianapolis. The Rule she adopted was the "primitive" one,[23] with its support for solitude and community. In the Constitutions she upholds the Rule and applies it to her understanding of reformed Carmelite life. These two documents guided the young Indianapolis community in every way: the hours of silence and prayer, the diet, times for rising and sleeping, penance, instruction of novices, care for the sick, and burial of the dead.

In the small quarters that constituted the first building phase of the Carmelite monastery of Indianapolis, the sisters lived according to those documents. The discipline required—to abstain from meat, to observe fasting for several months of the year, to sleep relatively little, and to work hard—was not designed to be easy, but was meant to be a joy, an adventure toward union with God in a loving community. "All must be friends, all must be loved, all must be held dear, all must be helped," Teresa told her sisters (*Way* 4.7). These few pioneers creating the foundation in Indianapolis were, by all accounts, described by these words. Their early lives were difficult—marked by the death of Mother Theresa and the fragility of Sister Hilda—but their resolve was firm. The expansion of the building in 1936 created the physical space for a larger community. As that building was underway, the young sisters, on their own in a new place, followed the Rule, immersed themselves in prayer, and waited patiently for the Lord.

Notes

1 She tells the story of this foundation in her *Life*. Jodi Bilinkoff gives her readers a genuine feel for Teresa's Avila, the reasons for secrecy, and the hostility of townspeople. See Bilinkoff, *The Avila of Saint Teresa: Religious Reform in a Sixteenth-Century City* (Ithaca: Cornell University Press, 1989).

2 See Bilinkoff, pp. 41-43.

3 Today this ancient prayer of the church is called the Liturgical Hours. The term "Divine Office" refers to a duty accomplished for God, specifically certain prayers recited at fixed hours by priests, members of religious orders, and any others who have vowed to keep them. It has a number of historical forms and usually includes Matins and Lauds (said in the morning), the so-called "little hours" of Prime, Terce, Sext, and None (said throughout the day), and Vespers and Compline (said in the evening).

4 The five sisters were Mother Theresa of the Trinity (Emma Seelbach), the prioress; Sister Hilda of Divine Providence (Hilda Ammann); Sister Miriam of the Child Jesus (Miriam Elder); Sister Agnes of Jesus (Genevieve Costello); and Sister Anne of the Trinity (Elizabeth Clem). Mother Theresa would have a heart attack three years later, leaving a shaky Sister Hilda in charge of three young sisters.

5 Simon-Guillaume-Gabriel Bruté de Remur came from an old and distinguished French family. He studied medicine and eventually became a priest (1808). He sailed for the United States in 1810 with the newly

appointed Bishop Joseph Flaget, who served the newly created diocese of Bardstown (later Louisville) until 1850. Bruté taught philosophy at Mount Saint Mary's Seminary until 1815, then was president of Saint Mary's College in Baltimore until 1834, when he was appointed to the Vincennes diocese. In 1816 Bruté wrote to the Carmelites in Paris on behalf of the Sisters in Baltimore and in return received relics of Teresa of Avila for them. See *Carmel: Its History, Spirit, and Saints*, Compiled from Approved Sources by The Discalced Carmelites of Boston and Santa Clara (New York: P. J. Kenedy and Sons, 1926), p. 149.

6 Bishop Chatard was directed to live in Indianapolis even though the cathedral and title of the See was still located in Vincennes. In a papal brief dated March 28 , 1898, Leo XIII changed the name of the diocese to Indianapolis.

7 Ritter was named auxiliary bishop of Indianapolis in 1933, and became its bishop in 1934. Ten years later he was named the first archbishop. He was transferred to St. Louis in 1946, and became a cardinal there in 1961. The new archbishop of Indianapolis was Paul Schulte, who arrived in the city on October 7, 1946.

8 See Sally Thompson, "The Problem of the Cistercian Nuns in the Twelfth and Early Thirteenth Centuries," in *Medieval Women*, ed. Derek Baker (Oxford: Basil Blackwell, 1978), pp. 227-352.

9 The original rules for religious orders in the early church and Middle Ages were written by and for men. When these orders accepted women as members, they adapted their Rule for them, writing, in effect, a "Second Rule" for women. Women following this Rule were under the jurisdiction of men within the order. "Third Order" refers to a "Third Rule" written for secular lay people who wish to be associated with a religious order and to make simple vows or promises according to their states in life. Today's Carmelites have dropped this "Second Order" language to describe sisters, and rather than having a "Third Order" have OCDS (Secular Order of Discalced Carmelites).

10 The Beguines were "arguably the most creative [form] of the important new styles of religious life adopted by women in the twelfth and thirteenth centuries . . . the only new form of 'apostolic life' in which women took the leadership role." See Bernard McGinn, ed., *Meister Eckhart and the Beguine Mystics* (New York: Continuum, 1997), pp. 2f.

11 See Joachim Smet, O.Carm, *The Carmelites: A History of the Brothers of Our Lady of Mount Carmel*, vol. I, *Ca. 1200 A.D. until the Council of Trent*, chapters VI and VII (Private printing, 1975; rev. ed. 1988).

12 Georges Bernanos wrote the libretto for this opera, inspired by a novel by Gertrude Von le Fort, *Die letzte am Schafott* (1931).

13 *How Buildings Learn: What Happens After They're Built* (New York: Viking Press, 1994). He is concerned with various aspects of adaptive architecture (planning for change, e.g., in initial designs).

14 From above, the four towers appear to be identical, but they are not. The one on the northwest corner is a "dummy" built for symmetry; its sister on the southwest corner opens inward to accommodate a small office in the Council Room on the second floor, and opens outward as a small "retreat space" on the first floor. The two turrets on the east side are air vents that open only on the first floor, where they are used as storage space.

15 The shield of Carmel contains a cross and three stars that refer to the glory of Carmel undimmed since the beginning of the Christian era: the three stars stand for Carmel in its Greek, Latin, and Western eras. A hand with a torch reminds us of God's fiery intervention at the behest of Elijah on Mount Carmel. The twelve surrounding stars symbolize twelve points of the Rule: obedience, chastity, poverty, recollection, mental prayer, Divine Office, chapter, abstinence, manual labor, silence, humility, and works of supererogation.

16 Ronald Knox's translation is a little more poetic: "I am all jealousy for the honour of the Lord God of Hosts."

17 Technically referred to as the "transverberation," this experience is described by Teresa in her *Life*, chapter 29, section 13. This is the experience that Giovanni Bernini (1598-1680) tried to capture in his baroque statue of Saint Teresa. It stands in the Cornaro Chapel of the Church of Santa Maria della Vittoria in Rome.

18 This shrine was put into storage in the years following the second Vatican council, and in October 1988 it was donated to the museum at the Shrine of the Little Flower in Darien, Illinois.

19 At the end of that hallway there is now the statue of Saint Thérèse of Lisieux that was formerly in the shrine/visiting room. In 1932, however, there was a door to the sacristy at the end of that hallway. The two doors on the left side led into the chapel, where one would see no statues or vigil lights, but an altar framed on both sides by the grille behind which the sisters attended Mass. A small opening in the wall is where the sisters came to receive communion.

20 Monasteries often had three kinds of sisters within them. Choir nuns were obligated to say the Divine Office at the appointed hours and spent a good deal of time practicing and learning rubrics. Lay sisters were cloistered but were freed from singing the Office so that they could attend to household tasks. Extern sisters were not cloistered: they acted as liaisons between the cloistered sisters and the outside world. Although Carmelite nuns did not sing the Office using elaborate Gregorian chant modes—Teresa wanted to free them from burdensome music practice and so specified a monotone chant style—they did have choir sisters and lay sisters. The Carmelites of Indianapolis never had extern sisters.

21 In that hallway were three cells, workrooms, and a bathroom. There was also a temporary stairway that the sisters used to get to the chapel, meeting rooms, and workrooms inside the house.

22 That door was sealed off in 1961, when the permanent chapel and choir were built. A hand-wrought iron crucifix donated by the Main family now hangs on the wall where the door to the shrine once was. It is inscribed on the back: "Eternal Father, we offer Thee the wounds of Our Lord, Jesus Christ in thanksgiving for the gift of our sweet mother, Hope Brown Main in whose dear memory this crucifix is lovingly given by her devoted children, Ruby Main Adams, Vera Main Boggs, and Palmer Main."

23 Not the original "Rule" of Albert, but the slightly modified Rule approved by Pope Innocent IV in 1247.

3 Content with Little

This chapter examines poverty, its place as a religious virtue in Christianity and in monastic life, and Teresa of Avila's conversion from a life of comfort to one of simplicity. I then connect Teresa's understanding of poverty to her insights about prayer and detachment before I move to the experience of the young sisters in the Indianapolis Carmel. Finally, we see the construction of the second phase of the building and get a look at Carmelite life in Indianapolis as it began to flourish and attract people to its public novenas and its private life from 1936 to 1941.

IMITATING CHRIST

From the earliest days of the Christian movement, disciples have sought to follow Christ as closely as possible. Early Christians met regularly to break bread as Jesus had done. Martyrs followed him to torturous deaths, sharing his agonies in their own bodies. When Constantine issued his decree ending the persecution of Christians and set about to endow Christian churches, to make them resplendent monuments to divine power and imperial majesty, some Christians sought a more radical way to express their beliefs and their love for God. Early Christian hermits fled to deserts, isolated rocky cliffs, and other remote areas in order to avoid the temptations of the world, the flesh, and the devil. In the language of early monasticism, they vowed themselves to poverty (against the blandishments of worldly success), to chastity (lest the lures of sexual love distract them from the pursuit of union with God), and to obedience (to discipline the will against self-centeredness). These three vows—called the "counsels of perfection" in Christian tradition—formed the backbone of religious life. People "in the world" might be prayerful and compassionate, but they could never quite be "perfect" as that concept was understood in the ancient world.[1] Perfection meant unreserved following of Christ: early monks and nuns were pilgrims of the absolute.

The concept of poverty was not simple. One can see already in the Gospel accounts of the Sermon on the Mount a tension between being "poor" (Luke) and being "poor in spirit" (Matthew). Clement of Alexandria, an early church father addressing more affluent populations, suggested that it was not riches that kept one from the kingdom of heaven, but undue attachment to them. The question was thus engaged and began to be played out in centuries of Christian history, and in that drama, hermits and monks were exemplars of holy poverty.

OPPOSITE: MOTHER ALOYSIUS HEIKER (BETTENDORF) AND MOTHER AGNES COSTELLO (INDIANAPOLIS), 1939
PREVIOUS SPREAD: PEOPLE ATTENDING NOVENA, C. 1948

As early monastic movements grew more successful and more endowed with wealth in the medieval period, reform movements called for monks to return to poverty. Francis of Assisi famously rejected his father's wealth and ran away to the outskirts of town to pray and live on whatever scraps people were willing to give him. His radical witness attracted followers and critics, and shortly after his death, his Franciscan brothers sought to soften the stringent claims of their founder. According to the earliest Carmelite legislation, "none of the brothers should call anything his own, but you shall hold all things in common,"[2] an evocation of the community of goods found in the *Acts of the Apostles*. By Teresa's time, however, the concept of holy poverty would have been unrecognizable to those first Carmelites.

TERESA'S EXPERIENCE

Teresa de Ahumada y Cepeda was the child of minor Spanish nobility. Her paternal grandfather was a wealthy *converso* merchant[3] who had managed to achieve the status of a nobleman with its honorific title of Don. As the child of parents made rich by the wool trade, Teresa was accustomed to good things (especially finely woven cloth). When she entered *la Encarnación* in 1535, it was one of the largest monasteries in the city and a center for the upper classes. Women who became nuns there were prepared to sing the Divine Office daily, but they had no intention of relinquishing their privileges (honorific titles, servants, and relatively palatial living quarters). In a house where poor sisters lived in dormitories, Teresa had a large private apartment, including facilities for cooking and eating, that was laid out on two floors with a connecting staircase. Several of her relatives lived with her, and she attracted a circle of friends who met in her rooms to chat and exchange gossip.

Teresa was apparently witty and a great companion. Wealthy ladies in the city begged for her company, and she seems to have made extended visits to the homes of rich patrons. The need to keep patrons happy, along with Teresa's own increasing scruples about the way in which she was living religious life, eventually led to her insistence that her reformed monasteries be founded in poverty. In order to free her sisters to pursue the path of solitary prayer—an approach to God that required hours of quiet reflection—she wanted her monasteries to rely on alms freely given, not on endowments provided by rich patrons. Her desire for poverty—awakened in her by saintly figures such as Peter of Alcantara and stimulated by the example of various reform-minded men and women in Avila[4]—was an attempt to break the connection between patronage and prayer as she had come to understand it. Whereas endowments mandated vocal commemorative prayers, a kind of spiritual busy work, alms supported prayer, the solitary adventure of a soul moving toward union with God.

In the complex choreography of medieval church/state relations, rich people who gave money or land to the church expected to have some control over it. Ecclesiastical officials who received these gifts just as surely fought to retain their own autonomy and control. In late medieval Avila, aristocrats dominated monastic foundations: they not only gave them land and money, they gave them detailed lists of duties that the monks or nuns would have to follow in order to "repay" their patronage. For example, at *la Encarnación*, nuns were obligated to the generosity of Bernardo Robles, who left the monastery an impressive endowment in his 1513 will. Although his money allowed them to build a main chapel and to pay off some substantial debts, it also obligated the sisters. "In exchange for this endowment Robles specified in minute detail how and where he was to be buried, and required that one nun continually kneel before the Blessed Sacrament, holding a candle in her hand, and pray for his soul. He placed his heirs in charge of the money, ordering them to withhold payments if the nuns should fail to carry out his request."[5] No doubt Teresa herself, as a nun in this monastery, participated in this arrangement.

The whole system was bound up with issues clustered around honor: who lived in the most prestigious neighborhoods, who had the right to walk first in processions, whose money was shiniest, whose blood was the most pure?[6] Founding religious houses was one way to add luster to one's honor, even as it guaranteed the patron an eternal method of prayer for the repose of his or her soul. Although the young Teresa participated in certain aspects of this Spanish obsession with honor—her family name, her title of Doña, her well-furnished apartment and fine cloth garments—she grew increasingly restive about it as she got older and was led by God to a different understanding of prayer. By the time she was ready to found the monastery of Saint Joseph's, therefore, she was fully dedicated to poverty. On the one hand, she was distressed with the ways in which wealth constrained behavior: for example, when she was sent to comfort Doña Luisa de Cerda in 1561, she was "tormented" by comforts and found herself "pitying" the rich.[7] On the other hand, she was increasingly convinced that God wanted her to found monasteries without endowments, so that sisters could pursue a life of solitary prayer supported only by alms freely given. Only in such a house would the sisters be free to explore "the way of perfection."[8]

Although Teresa had been thinking about making a small foundation for some time and was attracted to the concept of poverty, she was not sure that others would be. As she was involved in the practical intrigues of establishing Saint Joseph's, however, she was sent to Toledo, and there had ample time to consider her desire for poverty and to find new sources of support for it. While at the house of Doña Luisa, Teresa met Maria de Jesus, a *beata* who had founded a monastery in total poverty and who "was so far ahead of me in serving the Lord that I was ashamed" (*Life* 35.2). Maria de Jesus also seemed to know the primitive Rule of Carmel better than Teresa did, and told her that before the mitigation Carmelites had been ordered to own nothing. Although Teresa felt vindicated by this information, she was not quick to act on it. Typically, she sought advice from learned and holy men and found that they opposed the idea of a house founded without an endowment. Just as typically, Teresa turned to the Lord, "who told me I shouldn't in any way fail to found the monastery in poverty."[9]

Finally, Teresa did make her foundations without endowments, even as she recognized that the practicalities of poverty worked better in cities (where one could count on the support of many devout people) than in rural areas (where an impoverished monastery would put an undue strain on people's alms and good will). Some of the trials attached to unendowed monasteries can be found in her history of the foundations. She often began new monasteries in ramshackle houses that needed extensive cleaning and remodeling, work that she herself did with the help of her sisters. She once began in a dirty little house with two straw mattresses, a blanket, and a frightened young companion. Teresa's reformed monasteries, supported only with alms, were models of simple living. Her sisters ate no meat, slept on straw mattresses, had no adornments—tapestries, paintings, and statues—except in the chapel, and wore simplified habits made from coarse cloth.[10] When Teresa transferred her vows from the Incarnation to her new foundation at Saint Joseph's, she relinquished her title. No longer Doña Teresa, she was now simply Sister Teresa of Jesus.

CARMELITE POVERTY AND DETACHMENT

In the course of her own spiritual development, Teresa resolved to follow the "counsels of perfection." As she explained to her sisters in *The Way of Perfection*, two realities compelled her choice. On the one hand, the Lord had granted her great favors by inviting her into friendship and union; on the other hand, Christ was clearly suffering in the ravages of the Protestant Reformation and needed friends. She wanted to "do something" to support the sufferings of Christ, but she was not in a position to be effective in the world. She could, however, become a true friend of Christ by sharing His life as closely as possible: if it was true that God had so few friends, she reasoned, they must be good ones, totally loving, detached, and humble. At a time when men were braving the dangers of exploration and missionary work in the New World, or were putting their lives at risk in hostile religious territory in Europe, it looked as if women could do nothing. That was not Teresa's understanding: in a world that held women in low esteem, Teresa found courage and demanded it from her sisters. "I want you to be like strong men," she told them, able to withstand the demands of poverty (*Way* 7.8).

In addition to physical rigors, Carmelite life demanded interior asceticism, a poverty of spirit that was predicated on a particular understanding of freedom. Daily life was regulated by a detailed and omnipresent schedule that eliminated most choices, expected conformity, and required obedience in everything. Small acts of self-denial were taken for granted at each meal. There was very little leisure, no cultural pursuits, no friendships, and no decorative colors.[11] The days were spent in strict silence that was meant to be interior as well as exterior.

Nothing received (from families, for example) was kept, and the sisters had few personal possessions and no money. They cultivated great care and a conservative spirit in the use of things. Sisters were expected to cope with loneliness by seeking the companionship of Christ, and to see God's will manifest in the Rule and the words of their superiors. A nexus of liturgical, Carmelite, and Marian customs strengthened the community's life and made it possible for sisters to be free to pursue the kind of prayer that Teresa experienced.

Teresa believed that God invited all humanity toward union in prayer, but realized that most people did not have the time or determination to respond to that invitation. She understood God as a great monarch, and herself as the most unworthy of subjects. In the twenty years it took her to learn the lessons of contemplative prayer, she came to understand the total dedication God demanded for those who sought the intimacy that was possible through mental prayer. "This King doesn't give Himself but to those who give themselves entirely to Him," she told her sisters (*Way* 16.4). Continually throughout her writings, she insisted on love, detachment, and humility. Together they form the foundation on which a contemplative life can be built, but the gift of contemplation itself was God's to give. The poverty of life within the monastery was in some ways a metaphor for the poverty of spirit necessary for prayer. Only those truly detached from worries (about their diet, their health, their honor), determined to love God and their sisters, and able to welcome the bracing humility of self-knowledge, could be in a position to communicate fully with God. Such persons, she said, have no fear of anyone, for theirs is the kingdom of heaven. These virtues do not force God to lavish gifts upon those seeking union, but no union is possible without them. In the chess game of contemplative prayer, Teresa said, "there's no queen like humility for making the King surrender. Humility drew the King from heaven to the womb of the Virgin, and with it, by one hair, we will draw Him to our souls" (*Way* 16.2).

Detachment and poverty reinforced Teresa's teaching that contemplation is a gift, given freely by God as alms must be given freely by those who support monastic life. Contemplation is a special aspect of divine love, which is given because of who God is, not because of who we are. The only thing that one can give in this situation, where one acknowledges his or her inner poverty, is oneself. In concrete terms, in contemplative prayer, one gives one's time (refusing to be distracted by other things), determination (in the face of failure of disappointment), love (always receptive, willing to see everything as a grace), and humility (a contentment with what is). At its best, humility is self-knowledge, which for Teresa meant that she, a sinner who had often ignored God's overtures and yet was showered with God's favors, had to accept both painful realities (her sinfulness and her attractiveness to God). "Humility consists very much in great readiness to be content with whatever the Lord may want to do with [one] and in always finding oneself unworthy to be called His servant" (*Way* 16.6).

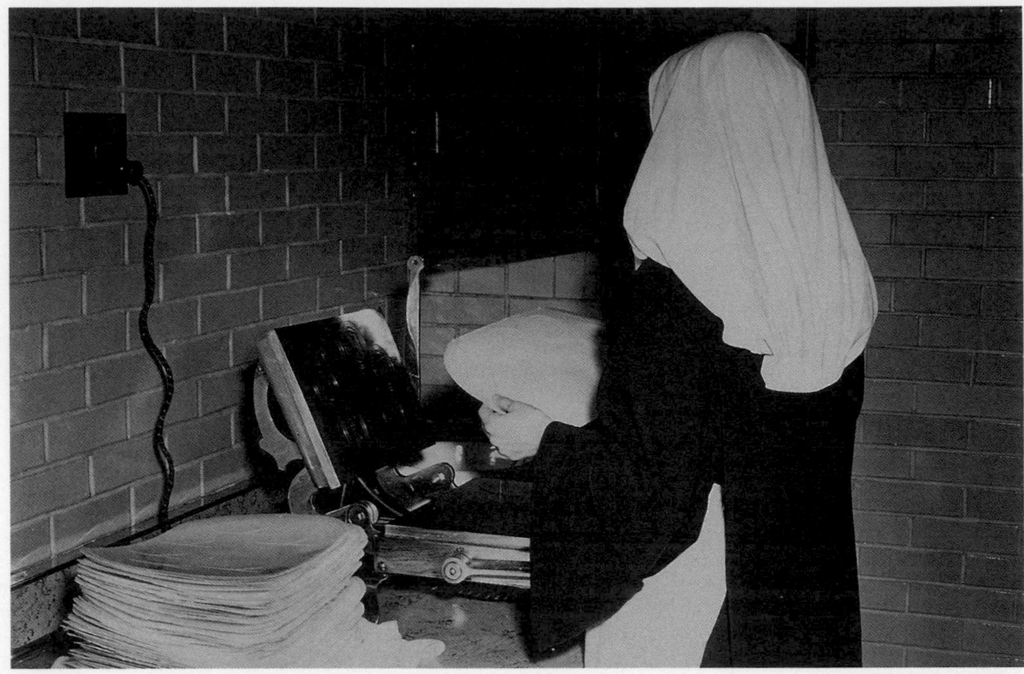

NOVICE BAKING ALTAR BREADS, C. 1941

THE POOR WOMEN OF INDIANAPOLIS

Paradoxically, poverty was meant to detach the sisters from worry by investing them with freedom of spirit. They were to work for results, but to be indifferent to them. The Rule and the customs that came to identify the daily life of Carmelite monasteries were designed to teach sisters a new language: "God is your business and language," Teresa told her sisters; "whoever wants to speak to you must learn this language" (*Way* 21.4). The young sisters in the monastery of Indianapolis did not have time to learn all the aspects of this language before Mother Theresa died. The early years in New Albany did not lend themselves to certain kinds of formation, so when they moved to Indianapolis in 1932, Miriam, Agnes, and Anne were not seasoned Carmelites. Although they were well grounded in Carmelite spirituality, they had never really learned the complicated ceremonials necessary for the proper recitation of the Divine Office. And they were still learning the myriad courtesies and duties of daily life when Mother Theresa Seelbach died in 1936. Because this situation was not able to be addressed during the tenure of Mother Hilda, Miriam, Agnes, and Anne in 1938 were rather like some of the nuns in Teresa's foundations, on their own in an unfinished building trying to figure out how to live the Carmelite Rule.

At first, these three young American Carmelites wrote to several different monasteries, asking each one a different question in an effort to figure things out, but in 1939 they

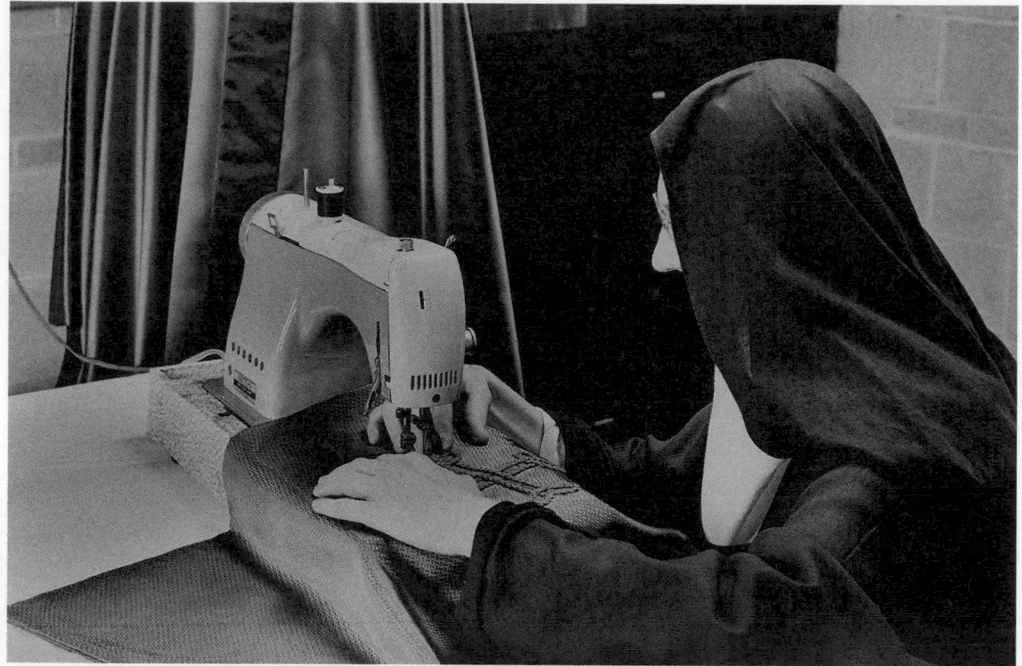

SISTER MAKING VESTMENTS, C. 1962

turned to Mother Aloysius of the Bettendorf Carmel. She and her companion, Sister Emmanuel, came to Indianapolis in early October and stayed with the young community for four months. By the time Mother Aloysius returned to Iowa, the sisters in Indianapolis knew the intricacies of their vocation. They were ready for the burgeoning of new life that would, in the twenty years before the second Vatican council, lead to two new foundations and support the spiritual quest of a lively community of women whose lives of simplicity were abundantly rich in spiritual gifts.

Along with the intricacies of Carmelite life, they understood poverty. Teresa believed that a rich interior life was incompatible with comfort and riches. Christ called them to lives of physical hardship, where their days were highly regulated and quietly heroic. Daily life in this twentieth-century monastery was not much different from that lived by Teresa and her sisters in the sixteenth century. Members of the small community of Indianapolis survived on six hours of sleep (rising by 5:00 A.M. and not retiring until 11:00 P.M.) and followed the most rigorous fasting rules in the church (only one full meal each day, no meat, no eating between meals).[12] Each day they recited the Divine Office with its specified hours of prayer; spent two hours in private, solitary prayer; did spiritual reading; and participated in the regular activities of community life (work, recreation, study, and household tasks). In addition, they took time for annual private retreats and days of recollection.

BUILDING FOR THE FUTURE

While it is true that holy men of India wander around existing on whatever food pious people deign to give them, and while it is true that Teresa needed to disconnect the path of prayer from the demands of patronage, monasteries need money. Construction and maintenance, whether for a home or a monastery, are costly. The simple needs of daily living and the extraordinary expenses of medical bills require well-managed capital. Most Carmelite monasteries, including the Carmel of the Resurrection in Indianapolis, were supported partly by the generosity of lay people, and partly by investing the dowries brought in by entering sisters.[13] But the vow of poverty is predicated on the willingness to support oneself with the work of one's hands, a tradition as old as the apostles. The Carmelite sisters of Indianapolis had three kinds of work in their early years: they made altar breads, designed and tailored vestments and altar cloths, and had a small calligraphy business. The altar bread business began almost as soon as the sisters moved into the Indianapolis monastery, and has been a steady source of income since then. It is labor-intensive work requiring sensitive measurements of ingredients and oven temperature, followed by cutting the hosts and then inspecting and packing them by hand, mailing them out to parishes, and keeping accounts. Although sisters made the vestments used in the monastery, they did not decide to make that work part of their financial support until 1954. The vestments created for the monastery and for other churches are magnificent examples of ornate and intricate design; they are no longer in fashion, but this line of work was an important income-producing source for many years. No monastery can exist without generating some income, and the sisters have worked steadily all their lives to support themselves even as they were recipients of generous donations from friends.

MIRIAM, AGNES, AND ANNE, C. 1938

The first wing of the monastery in Indianapolis cost $142,000, money that the sisters had to find (through donations or bank loans). The second wing, begun in July 1936 and finished in January 1937, cost an additional $15,000. This second building project, a small addition to the south wing, was built under the supervision of Emil Zurschmied, the young man who had helped Mother Theresa remodel the New Albany house into the first temporary monastery in the 1920s. In July 1936, when the caretakers of the monastery resigned, Mr. Zurschmied and his family moved to Indianapolis, where they assisted the sisters for the next twenty years. The sec-

OPPOSITE: ROCK CLIFF IN FRONT OF MONASTERY, 1939

ARCHITECT SKETCHES, WROUGHT-IRON RAILINGS FOR FRONT STEPS (1932)

VI CORPUS CHRISTI/7TH STEP CHI/RHO, FIRST TWO LETTERS IN CHRISTOS (GREEK FOR CHRIST)
III PASCHAL TIME/4TH STEP SUNRISE, SYMBOL OF THE RISEN CHRIST

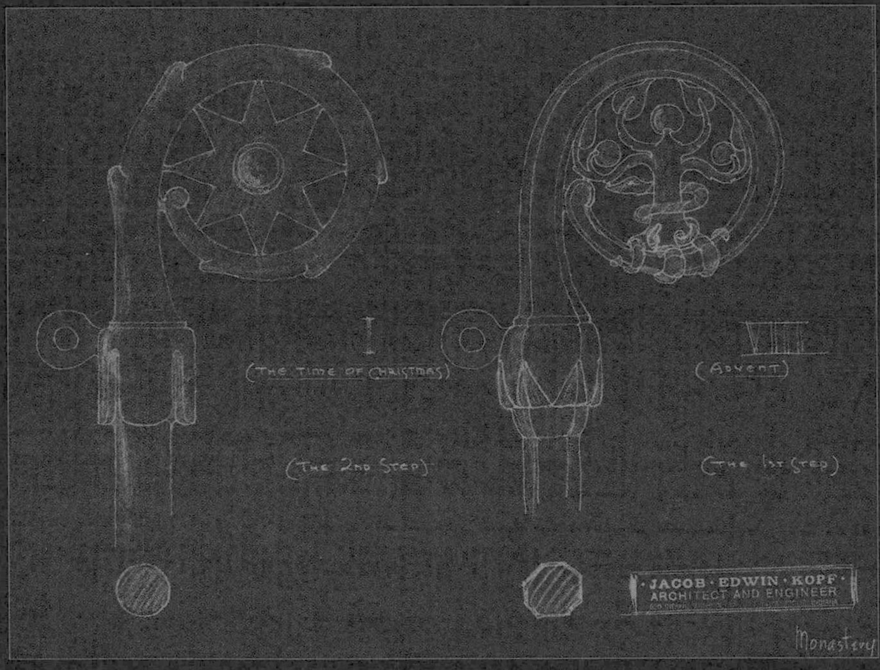

I TIME OF CHRISTMAS/2ND STEP STAR OF BETHLEHEM HAILS THE BIRTH OF CHRIST
VIII ADVENT/1ST STEP JESSE TREE, TRADITIONAL ADVENT SYMBOL

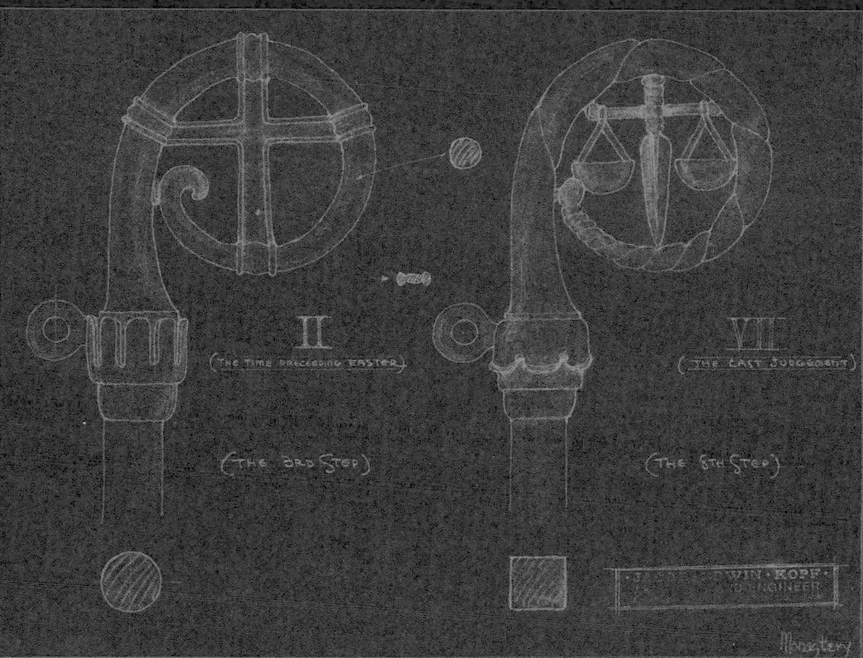

II TIME PRECEDING EASTER/3RD STEP CROSS REMINDER THAT LENT IS A SEASON OF PENANCE
VII THE LAST JUDGMENT/8TH STEP SCALES OF JUSTICE

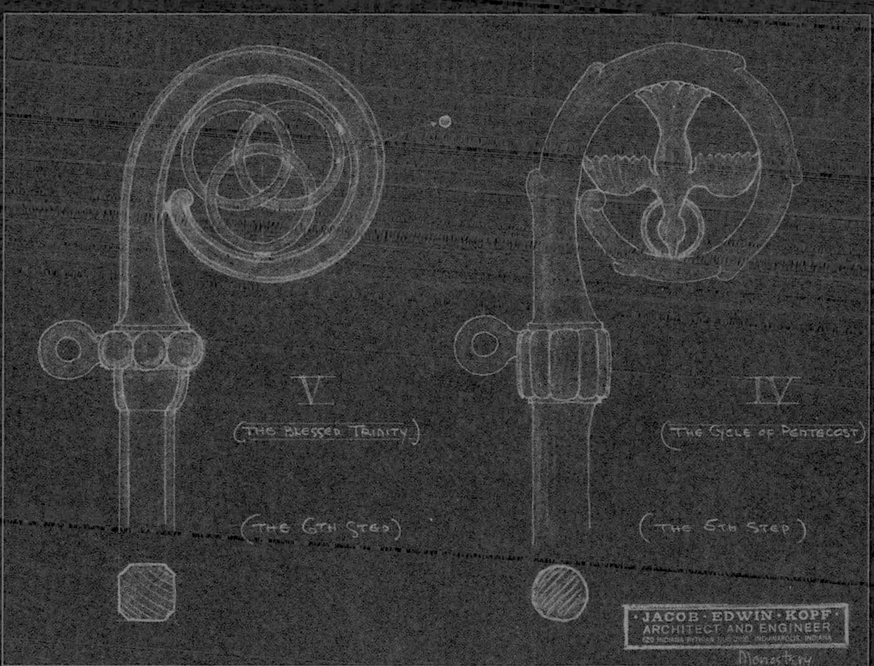

V THE BLESSED TRINITY/6TH STEP SYMBOL OF THREE PERSONS IN ONE GOD
IV THE CYCLE OF PENTECOST/5TH STEP DESCENT OF THE HOLY SPIRIT ON APOSTLES

ond phase of the building project was relatively straightforward. The western end of the south wing had been boarded up until there were sufficient funds to continue building. Those barriers were now removed, and six new cells and two bathrooms were added on the second floor. On the first floor, more storage space and workrooms were built. The original plans included designs for every aspect of those rooms; for example, cabinets and drawers were specifically designed for particular items of clothing.

The rooms, however, were only part of the "building" that occurred in those years. Between 1936, when this small addition was begun, and 1941, when the third building phase was begun, the community began to grow in numbers, and the prayerful presence of the sisters in the city began to take shape. Two visible signs of that growth were the landscaping project of 1938 and the initiation of the annual outdoor novenas in 1939.

The landscaping project was designed to create a "cliff" in front of the house. Before she died, Mother Theresa discussed her plans for the front embankment with Mr. Kopf. The monastery should look as if it had been built on an elevation, she thought, and a welcoming front yard with a graceful driveway should provide a way for the people of Indianapolis to participate in some of the prayerful aspects of the monastery's life. In 1938, the front of the property was graded and the "cliff" was built. Dennis Bush, a retired road commissioner and friend of the sisters, supervised the grading project under the architectural direction of Jacob Kopf and the landscaping expertise of the Hillsdale Nursery. Once the large pile of soil was in place, Mr. Zurschmied used horses to drag large stones from the property, along with some donated by the hospital across the street, and put them in place so that they appeared to be the outcroppings of a cliff. When approaching the monastery on the curved front drive, therefore, people saw (as they see today) a large rock formation to the south of the main front stairway. At the bottom of this stairway, the hand-wrought iron lamppost that had been part of the original design was installed, and along the balustrade, a series of wrought iron pillars topped with Catholic symbols.[14] These finishing touches were both beautiful and practical. The "cliff" was built both for effect—setting the monastery dramatically above the road—and to serve as the focal point for the annual novena.

THE COMMUNITY, C. 1940

PEACOCK GATE AT MONASTERY ENTRANCE

From July 8th to 16th, 1939, the first novena to Our Lady of Mount Carmel was celebrated on the monastery grounds. Father Francis Lyons, a Paulist priest, led the nine-day prayer service, a boys' choir provided music for the nightly celebration of the Benediction of the Blessed Sacrament, and the thousands of people who attended sat on lawn chairs or on blankets to listen to preaching and participate in the novena prayers. By all accounts, between two and three thousand were there each evening, and four thousand on the last night. The July novena was celebrated annually until 1974, with a small altar, a lectern, and an amplification system set up on a wooden platform on the top of "the cliff."[15] Before the 1940 novena, the impressive peacock gates and lanterns were installed at each end of the drive.[16]

Although thousands attended the novenas each year, the sisters, enclosed in their sacred space, were not permitted to leave the cloister to attend them. Their prayer was of a different kind. In the calculus of religious life, those dedicated to solitary prayer were required to make a radical separation from "the world" even when part of that world was praying in their front yard. Carmelite spirituality had its roots in an ancient and paradoxical desire. Biblical figures such as Moses, Elijah, and the psalmist all longed to see God face to face even as they knew that "no one may see the face of God and live." Behind their cloistered walls, the sisters played out various aspects of this paradox. They sought a freedom of spirit within a system of constraints, hoping to find joy in lives dedicated to penance, and to find in poverty the treasures of heaven.

Notes

1 In the Gospels, Jesus tells a rich young man that in order to be "perfect" he must sell all he has, give the money to the poor, and come follow Him. See Matthew 19.16-22. That demand, along with the example of Christ willing to give His life for the redemption of the world, was taken as a mandate for total Christian life by some ancient interpreters.

2 Michael Mulhall, O.Carm, ed., *Albert's Way: The First North American Congress on the Carmelite Rule* (Barrington, Ill.: The Province of the Most Pure Heart of Mary, 1989), pp. 7, 9.

3 Although Jews, Christians, and Muslims had coexisted for centuries in medieval Spain, non-Christians from the fifteenth century onward were increasingly persecuted. Jews were expelled from the Iberian Peninsula in 1492, and Moors in the early sixteenth century. Before the great expulsions, however, Jews had been increasingly harassed and forced to convert to Christianity. The term *converso* refers to converted Jews. Teresa's grandfather, Juan Sanchez, was a *converso* in Toledo who was denounced to the Inquisition in 1485 for returning to Jewish practices. After doing public penance for several weeks, he removed his family to Avila and there used wealth, connections, and lawsuits "to establish relations with Avila's important families . . . and [won] the status of a gentleman." Jodi Bilinkoff, *The Avila of Saint Teresa: Religious Reform in a Sixteenth-Century City* (Ithaca: Cornell University Press, 1989), pp. 109-11.

4 She writes eloquently about Peter (1499-1562), an ascetic Franciscan priest canonized in 1669, in her *Life*, chapter 27. When, eventually, she found herself wavering on founding her monasteries in poverty, he appeared to her in a vision and insisted on it. For more on the reform atmosphere and personalities of Avila during Teresa's lifetime, see Bilinkoff.

5 See Bilinkoff, pp. 50-51. She describes the terms of the will and says that this kind of check by patrons was not unusual.

6 An obsession in Spain at this time was the *limpieza de sangre*, "purity of blood," meaning those Spaniards whose families had no "taint" of Jewish or Moorish blood. Teresa's Jewish ancestry and her eventual distress with the whole concept of honor account for the fact that her convents did not deny membership to *conversos*.

7 See her *Life*, chapter 34. Just as she was planning to found Saint Joseph's, she was sent to comfort this new widow and had occasion to notice the burdens of wealth.

8 *The Way of Perfection*, one of Teresa's most accessible works, was written for her nuns within a few years of her founding of the monastery of Saint Joseph's. It is a practical book, instructing the sisters about prayer and explaining (in the first chapters) her thoughts on poverty.

9 See *Life*, chapter 35. For an account of the opposition to poverty and the strain that it would put upon the city of Avila, see Bilinkoff.

10 These specifications, found in the Constitutions and scattered throughout her works, are much different from her relatively comfortable life at the monastery of the Incarnation. And the coarse cloth was a radical departure from a life of finely woven garments provided by her wool merchant relatives. "Eventually fabric became for Teresa a tangible symbol of the vanities of the world. She would refer to unreformed Carmelites as religious 'of the cloth' (*del pano*)." See Bilinkoff, p. 114.

11 The sisters did not paint their cells until 1965.

12 During Lent, adult lay people in the Catholic church followed a mitigated form of this fast (one full meal each day, the other two not to amount to that one meal), and all Catholics over the age of seven were permitted meat at their main meal only. The sisters followed a stringent form of fasting for most of the year: From September 14 until Lent, they had two pieces of bread and coffee in the morning, a full meal (no meat) at noon, and twelve ounces of something (fruit, vegetables, bread) for supper. From Lent to Easter and all

Fridays, they observed a "black fast," which prohibited all milk, eggs, butter, and cheese: two pieces of bread for breakfast, a regular meal at noon, and eight ounces of something (fruit, vegetables, bread) for supper. In 1954, the fasting laws changed so that the "black fast" was optional. The sisters in Indianapolis, however, observed it until the late 1960s. Today some are vegetarians, some are not.

13 Although some of the sisters who joined Teresa's reform movement brought dowries with them, in accordance with monastic requirements of the time, she would not refuse entry to those who could not provide that financial support. At the monastery in Indianapolis, some women entered with dowries that were invested toward the future, and some did not.

14 The symbols, each mounted on a differently designed post, are meant to take the stair climber through the liturgical and doctrinal moments of Catholic life. Beginning at the bottom step, the symbols are Advent, Christmas, Lent, Paschal time, Pentecost, the Trinity, Corpus Christi, and the Last Judgment.

15 Ironically, shortly after the sisters had a concrete slab poured in this space and wired so that a sound system could be easily used there, the novenas ceased to attract sizable crowds.

16 Peacocks are a symbol of the resurrection, and so an apt design for this "Carmel of the Resurrection." The gates were designed by Jacob Kopf and were built and installed by Meierjohan-Wengler Inc. of Cincinnati.

RING BELL
WALK IN DOOR
TO THE RIGHT

4 Never Out/Never Seen

This chapter explores enclosure, its application to monastic life for women, and Teresa of Avila's embrace of cloistered life after many years in an unenclosed monastery. I explain why she thought cloister necessary for the life of prayer she envisioned for her sisters before I describe the building of the third wing of the monastery in 1941. As vocations increased, the Indianapolis monastery was in a position to establish new foundations in Terre Haute (1947) and Reno, Nevada (1954). Although life in the Indianapolis Carmel proceeded much as it had in Teresa of Avila's day, winds of change were in the air, and this chapter ends just before the last building project began in 1960, with some anticipation of the second Vatican council.

Enclosure in History

When early Christian men and women went to the desert to lead lives of ascetic seclusion, there was no concept of cloister. Pious men and women, though drawn to an eremitical life, visited the sick and talked with visitors even as they spent most of their days in prayer. In the early Middle Ages, double monasteries—men and women sharing a common life in separate houses on a single property, or in separate wings of a single house—were common.[1] Benedict, who wrote the first Rule for Western monasticism, required a vow of stability, but no enclosure.

Little by little, however, a concept of material enclosure evolved in Western Christianity. Monks were not allowed to go into convents, monasteries were required to be surrounded by walls, and a concept of enclosure that was gender-specific took shape. A Rule for nuns written by Caesarius of Arles in the middle of the sixth century was the first to impose cloister rules on women.[2] Still, there was no concept of grilles (latticed walls of separation) and no solidified concept of enclosure. By the thirteenth century, however, there was a general tendency to rigidify enclosure rules. At precisely the time when apostolic orders were founded, allowing religious men to wander through Europe preaching and witnessing to radical concepts of poverty, religious women were strictly enclosed. *Periculoso*, published by Boniface VIII in 1298, required strict enclosure for all nuns of every order, but set forth no equivalent legislation for monks.

Although *Periculoso* was not uniformly enforced, more and more orders of nuns were adopting rules of strict enclosure by the fourteenth century. Grilles were erected in chapels so that nuns were not able to see the priest at Mass; grilles were erected in visiting rooms so that contact with visitors was made in a metaphorical context of separation

OPPOSITE: VISITORS TO THE MONASTERY RANG THIS BELL UNTIL 1970
PREVIOUS SPREAD: NOVITIATE WING SEPARATED BY CHAINS, 1941

from the world. Nuns were forbidden to leave the cloister, a rule that carried a penalty of excommunication when the Council of Trent adopted it in 1562.

NUN IN GRATE VEIL, C. 1954

Before the second Vatican council in the early 1960s, the laws of enclosure were highly explicit. Enclosed nuns had to be isolated from the world, surrounded by high, thick walls. Their chapels were divided, with cloistered nuns attending Mass behind a latticed grille unseen by the public. When sisters answered the turn bell, they could not be seen, because the small door was covered with a curtain. If they had to meet a worker—someone to fix the plumbing, for example—and take him into the house, they wore a "grate veil" that covered their faces completely. Turns and grilles were fully specified, and guest quarters were supposed to be uncomfortable so that visitors would not be tempted to stay long. In some versions of the legislation, there were to be no outside windows, the nuns' garden was to conform to a precise and relatively small size, and there was to be no more than one entrance into the house. A prioress who admitted someone—a doctor, for example—without permission from the bishop could be excommunicated.

Throughout the twentieth century, these rules became increasingly specific: double iron grates in visiting rooms, opaque glass in windows, and no possibility for nuns to touch anyone from the outside.[3] Teresa's desire for enclosure and her writings about it are not this exact, but the intention to be closed away from the world is surely there. Although the Council of Trent ruled in 1562, about the time Teresa began her reform, that all nuns were to be strictly enclosed, this legislation was not readily accepted in Spain. As noted earlier, the Spanish crown was generally suspicious of and sometimes hostile to outside interference, even by the pope. When Teresa received papal permission to establish Saint Joseph's in 1562, she placed the house under the jurisdiction of the local bishop, Alvaro de Mendoza. He believed in her and her movement, but "may also have recognized that her monastic program expressed many of the values held by the Tridentine Fathers."[4] Her ideas of strict cloister, a limited number of nuns, a long and selective novitiate, and a minimum age of entrance were similar to the legislation of the Council of Trent. The idea of an enclosed monastery of nuns, therefore, which seemed a bizarre novelty to Teresa's sisters in *la Encarnación*, turned out to be in keeping with the mind of the church.

ENCLOSURE FOR TERESA

In *The Way of Perfection*, Teresa told her sisters that she was asking them not to do "something new" but simply to be true to the Rule. The spirit of Carmelite prayer, as expressed in the lives of the earliest Carmelites, was a constant listening to the inspired word of God in solitude: each friar was to stay in his cell "meditating on the Word of the Lord day and night." When Teresa founded her reformed monasteries in the spirit of the early Rule, therefore, she established houses of solitude in which the original eremitical aspects of the Rule could be affirmed in both individual and collective terms. Silence made prayer possible for individual sisters. With the exception of reciting the Divine Office and talking during daily recreation, sisters spent their days wrapped in silence. Enclosure protected the solitude of the community by keeping them away from the distractions of the world.

Late in December 1561, less than a year before she founded Saint Joseph's, Teresa wrote to her brother Lorenzo and told him what she was planning. The house would be small, she said, and the nuns "will practice a very strict enclosure and thus never go out or be seen without veils covering their faces. Their lives will be founded on prayer and mortification."[5] Later, when she wrote the Constitutions, she elaborated: a nun should never be seen with her face unveiled, should disregard the affairs of the world, should avoid conversation with relatives, and should be careful in speaking to outsiders.[6]

Teresa's embrace of enclosure was stimulated by her effort to accept God's love for her. In her *Life*, a text about struggle and conflict, she gives a vivid account of her failures and God's favors, her fears and God's reassurance, her weakness and God's strength. Rowan Williams, Anglican bishop and scholar of spirituality, says that the first ten chapters of the *Life* describe God's victory over Teresa's weakness, and that the remaining chapters "set out God's victory through Teresa's weakness over the skepticism and hostility of the religious establishment, and how this victory in turn overcomes Teresa's own doubts and scruples."[7] As she learned a new path of prayer and experienced God's active presence in her life, she saw that "perfection is not attained quickly," and that sanctity was a lone venture (*Life* 31.17, 20). As she considered what she could "do for God," she first thought only to keep the Rule as perfectly as possible, but soon was inspired to found a reformed monastery, one that was small, without endowment, and enclosed.

In spite of the fact that the papal legislation of 1298 decreed that all nuns everywhere were to be perpetually enclosed, the monastery that Teresa entered in 1535 had no vow of enclosure. When she decided to found her monasteries with a vow of enclosure, the nuns at *la Encarnación* took it as a rebuke. "I was very much disliked throughout my monastery," she says, "because I had wanted to found a more enclosed monastery. They said I was insulting them" (*Life* 33.2). In reporting the reactions of her sisters, she says that she had to remain silent in the face of their criticisms, unable to tell them that the Lord had commanded her to ensure enclosure in her monasteries.

Years later, as Teresa finished the book of her *Foundations*, she reflected on enclosure. "No one but those who experience it will believe the joy that is felt in these foundations once we are enclosed where no secular person can enter, for however much we love them it is not enough to take away this great consolation in finding ourselves alone. It seems comparable to taking many fish from the river with a net: they cannot live until they are in water again. So it is with souls accustomed to living in the running streams of their Spouse. When taken out of them and caught up in the net of worldly things, they do not truly live until they find themselves back in those waters" (*Foundations* 31.46). Teresa speaks here with fondness, and also, perhaps, some regret, since she was not able to live the enclosed life she longed for when she founded the monastery of San José in Avila. Indeed, she spent months and months on the road, negotiating with ecclesiastical and local officials, establishing small houses, directing her sisters, writing letters, and drafting the books that would become classics of Carmelite spirituality. Underneath the bustle, however, was someone who believed that God inhabits the deepest center of the soul and beckons to us through silence and solitude. Her instructions to her sisters about prayer were sometimes a gloss on her views about enclosure. Sisters should practice inward recollection, she said; "those who by such method can enclose themselves within this little heaven of our soul where the Maker of heaven and earth is present . . . should believe that they are following an excellent path" (*Way* 28.5). Silent, enclosed prayer was Teresa's way of perfection and a mandate for those who followed her, including the sisters in Indianapolis.

ARCHITECT'S PLAN FOR THE COMPLETED MONASTERY WITH ITS GREAT CHURCH

ADDING TO THE ENCLOSURE IN INDIANAPOLIS

An article in the *Indianapolis Star* in 1938 announced plans to build the great monastery church envisioned by Mother Theresa. It gave a detailed list of specifications about the proposed size of the nave, the aisles, and the choir grille. The lower floor was to have a tower with chimes, and the altar was going to be a magnificent creation of silver and blue. It was a grand plan, but it was not to be.

The existing monastery now had twelve cells, nine within the present cloister in the south wing and the three in the east wing that had been used by Miriam, Anne, and Agnes from 1932 to 1936. Because the monastery now had five sisters and several more women asking for entrance, the bishop decided that the planned church would have to wait until more cells were built. The revised building project, contracted in 1940, included plans for three new cells in the south wing and nine novitiate cells in the west wing, plus one full and one half bathroom.[8] New storage rooms and workrooms were built on the first floor, including a new laundry room, larger rooms for the baking, cutting, and storing of altar breads, and rooms to be used by the provisor (the sister in charge of the kitchen). Once the project was underway, it was clear that there would be enough money in the budget for the sisters to add a new, larger kitchen and refectory to the first floor as well. It was now possible for the builders to connect all the wings of the first floor so that the sisters could circumnavigate the entire monastery on that level. That option would not be available on the second floor until 1961.

FAÇADE FOR A GREAT CHURCH TO BE BUILT LATER, C. 1940

Although the grand church would never be built, the bishop did allow the sisters to build the entrance to the proposed church, with its turrets, stonework, and great oak doors. They then built a new "temporary chapel" behind that façade, a wooden structure that would serve the community until the permanent chapel was built in 1961. Construction on the new wing and new temporary chapel was begun in March 1941 and finished in February 1942. Sadly, Mr. Kopf, the architect who had been involved with the building project for more than a decade, died that year in March.

As the monastery began to take fuller shape, changes were made in the original structure. The first "temporary chapel" became a visiting room (with grilles and a turn), and the three cells in the east wing were remodeled into guest quarters, used, for the most

LEFT: CAPITAL IN COURT DEPICTS THE SACRAMENT OF CONFIRMATION; RIGHT: SISTERS BUILDING HERMITAGE, C. 1953

part, by retreat directors.[9] Rooms on the first floor that had been used for laundry, cooking, and eating were now used for a variety of other functions, such as ceramics (which the sisters once considered for income-producing work).

From the outside, one could not see many changes: the north turrets had been added, and the façade of what would, they hoped, eventually be the grand church now fronted a temporary chapel. From the inside, however, the sisters could now see the essential shape of a courtyard monastery. The interior "court" was surrounded by Corinthian-style pillars with elaborate capitals, designed and executed by Amilcare Marchetti, an Italian stonemason who set up a workroom in the space near the boiler room. Although the court pillars were put up as each section was completed, the floor around the courtyard was not poured until all construction was finished in 1961. When the central courtyard was finished, there were thirty-nine arches and sixteen pillars, all executed in what sisters remember as "Mr. Marchetti's shop." Half of the capitals have geometric patterns, but the other half are exquisite renditions of the sacramental symbols of the church.[10] By 1950, the court, adorned by these beautiful pillars, was also beginning to be overgrown: the graceful willow trees that had been planted there in 1932 had outgrown the space and were cut down by the sisters.

Although construction on the building was finished in 1942, a series of additional projects took nearly another decade to finish. For example, some of the land surrounding the building was enclosed behind a high stone wall. When the monastery was begun, its clois-

SISTERS CUTTING DOWN WILLOWS IN THE COURT, 1951

ter wall was wooden and encompassed only a relatively small space. After the west wing was finished, however, builders were able to enclose five acres behind a permanent cloister wall. By August 1951, the monastery had two kinds of permanent enclosed outdoor space: a courtyard within the monastery and a cloistered yard outside. Some of the building projects in this time frame were completed in that yard. The fish pond that the sisters dug out in November 1945—which was lined with concrete and stocked with fish from the Trappist monastery in Kentucky in 1946—was made even more beautiful by Our Lady of Mount Carmel. That six-foot-high statue, commissioned by the sisters with funds donated by friends, arrived in late August 1951 and was set into the wall overlooking the pond.[11] As if to mark these achievements with festivity, a new set of large bells arrived at the monastery and were installed in the court just outside the library. They were rung for the first time on August 29, 1951, for the veiling of Sister Francis of the Good Shepherd (Rosemary Crump), who entered the monastery in 1946.

Grounds, like buildings, have a life of their own and change over time. Once the exterior walls were finished, the sisters and Mr. Zurschmied constructed several small hermitages on the property, affording individual sisters yet another kind of enclosure as they took time to pray apart from the community. The desire behind all this enclosure was solitude, the space one needed to be present to a God whose desire for the soul was understood by Teresa in intimate terms. "I am not asking now that you think about Him or that

SISTERS WATERPROOFING SOUTH WALL OF MONASTERY, 1950

you draw out a lot of concepts or make long and subtle reflections with your intellect. I am not asking you to do anything more than look at Him," she told her sisters; "in the measure that you desire Him, you will find Him" (*Way* 26.3). In a Teresian metaphor for prayer, we are like straw that needs to keep close to the hearth waiting to catch fire. One draws near to God with strong determination made possible by silence in an enclosed community. Underneath her desire for enclosure was a lifetime of practice that convinced her that such intimacy was possible only in abiding solitude.

INTERIOR LIFE IN INDIANAPOLIS BEFORE THE SECOND VATICAN COUNCIL

Once the last part of the sisters' living quarters was completed in 1942, the life Teresa envisioned within a reformed monastery could proceed in relative peace. The sisters in the Carmelite monastery of Indianapolis would not begin another building program for nearly twenty years, and since those years occurred before Vatican II, they would unfold within the time-honored patterns set down by Teresa and embodied by Carmelite sisters all over the world. The daily schedule, rigorous fasting, and poverty within a small enclosed community continued as they had for centuries. Many young women came to try their vocations in this monastery during these years. Some stayed; others did not. In general, however, life within the Carmel of the Resurrection flourished, and the sisters found themselves facing a variety of challenges: during the war, they responded to a call for help from a European community, and after the war, the Indianapolis Carmel established two new foundations.

COMMUNITY BEFORE RENO FOUNDATION, 1954

In 1940, as World War II was menacing Europe, a small group of Dutch Carmelites living in Iceland wrote to the monastery in Indianapolis to tell them of their plight. American troops had taken over their monastery as a barracks, and the sisters needed somewhere to go. When the Indianapolis sisters told the bishop about this problem and their desire to help, he was apparently amused at the very thought of getting three sisters transported from Iceland in the middle of a full-scale war. When their situation grew more desperate, however, Mother Agnes, prioress of the Indianapolis monastery, relentlessly petitioned the United States government to help them. Finally, in 1943, three Dutch sisters—Mother Elizabeth and Sisters Veronica and Martina—packed a few belongings, boarded a United States Navy ship, and eventually arrived in Indianapolis. They stayed there from August of that year until late February 1944, when they moved to the Carmelite monastery in Newport (now Barrington), Rhode Island.[12] By August 1945 they were safely back home in Iceland, and the sisters in Indianapolis duly celebrated their return to their own monastery and the end of the war. As life returned to normal, the sisters embarked upon a new adventure, the establishment of a foundation, a "daughter house."

Because religious life has traditionally been a compelling witness and an attractive option, it has flourished. In its earliest years, eremetical life was such a stunning response to the success of imperial Christianity that hundreds of young men and women were drawn to it. Religious orders that began with a single monastery eventually grew into enormous systems, hundreds of "daughter houses" linked together by a common observance. The impulse to make foundations, therefore, was part of the very life force of the Carmelite reform, and it was natural that when the time was ripe, the Indianapolis sisters would also seek to make new foundations.

Teresa's original idea involved the founding of one reformed house, Saint Joseph's, where she hoped to spend the rest of her days in quiet contemplation. As she says in the first chapter of the *Foundations*, "the five years I spent in Saint Joseph's in Avila after its foundation seem to me to have been the most restful of my life, and my soul often misses that calm and quiet" (*Foundations* 1.1). When some missionaries from the New World visited her, however, and described their heroic work, she was inspired to "do more" for God. That desire, almost immediately upheld by the Lord, led her to found fourteen additional reformed monasteries, twelve for women and two for men. By the time of her death, seventeen small reformed houses for women had been established in Spain. Later, her flourishing movement was taken first to France and then to Belgium by Anne of Saint Bartholomew (Teresa's nurse and companion) and Anne of Jesus. From the monasteries of English Antwerp and Hoogstraten, both in Belgium, a group of Carmelites founded the first monastery in the United States, at Port Tobacco (later Baltimore). And, as noted earlier, Baltimore established the foundation in Iowa that was the "mother house" of the Indianapolis Carmel.

When the fifteen sisters in Indianapolis first considered a foundation, they hoped to establish a new monastery in Chicago. For a number of reasons, however, they were persuaded by the bishop to make their first foundation in Terre Haute, Indiana, instead. The plan in 1945 was similar to the one Teresa herself had used throughout Spain. The sisters had to find an appropriate house, remodel it into an enclosed monastery, and then send a few sisters there to begin Carmelite life in a new place. The "mother house" was responsible for providing furnishings and finding the initial funding for the project, and the records from 1945 and 1946 contain receipts for the many things that were needed to pro-

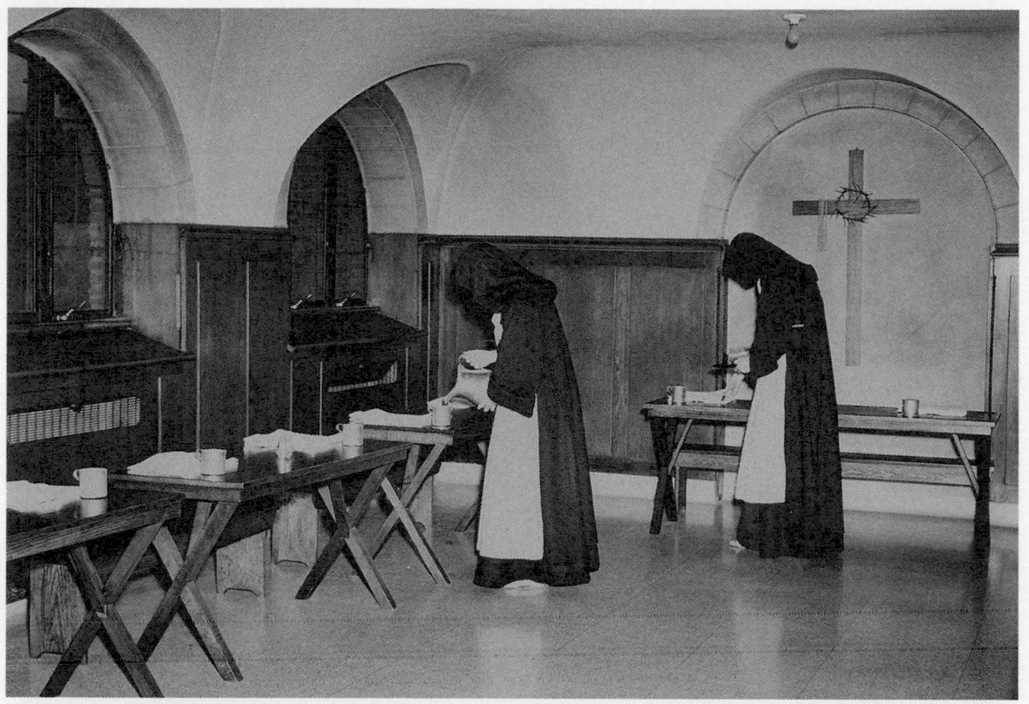

TOP: REFECTORY (DINING ROOM), C. 1952. SISTERS ATE IN SILENCE FACING CENTER. BOTTOM: REFECTORY (DINING ROOM) C. 1975, REDESIGNED SO THAT MEALS COULD BE A TIME FOR SHARING.

FISH POND INSIDE ENCLOSURE WALL, 1959

vide the stuff of monastic life there. On October 7, 1947, Mother Agnes Costello and six other sisters from Indianapolis moved to Terre Haute to begin life in the second Carmelite monastery in the Indianapolis archdiocese.[13] Their departure necessitated new elections in the Carmel of the Resurrection, and in 1947, as the sisters celebrated their silver jubilee (the New Albany foundation began in 1922), they elected Sister Miriam Elder, the first woman to enter in New Albany and remain with the community, as their new prioress. That same year, Father Raymond Bosler was appointed as their chaplain.

The loss of seven sisters to a new foundation was quickly made up in the next few years as many young women entered the Carmel of the Resurrection. The 1950s, sometimes remembered as the golden age of religious vocations in this country, were a time of stability and new life for the monastery. They were also years that saw some physical improvements (to the roof and the parapets) and additions (a shower was installed in the guest quarters in 1952) and some new ideas. For example, older sisters were now allowed to read *America* and *Commonweal*, two distinguished Catholic magazines that kept the sisters apprised of events and ideas in the church. The sisters designed and printed their first brochure in 1954, and in 1955 Mother Grace opened the library to the community, allowing the sisters more latitude in their choice of reading material. The church was making some changes as well: revised fasting laws permitted communicants to drink water up to one hour before receiving, and the traditional "black fast" was abolished.

By 1953, the community was again large enough to consider making a foundation, this one planned for Reno, Nevada. As with Terre Haute, the sisters had first to find, remodel, and furnish a house in the area, and then send sisters to begin the foundation there. Sister Angela Macy, Sister Anne Clem, and six other sisters from Indianapolis made their way west to begin the Reno foundation.[14] They were enclosed there on August 11, 1954. The two Indianapolis foundations eventually embodied two different styles as they responded to the spirit and challenges of the second Vatican council. The sisters in Terre Haute stayed with the traditional face of Carmel, maintaining certain signs of that tradition, including strict enclosure and the habit designed by Teresa. The nuns in Reno, like their sisters in the "mother house" in Indianapolis, found dynamic possibilities in enclosure, modified the traditional habit, and eventually adopted lay clothes.

The 1950s were times of new life for the monastery, in terms of both community members and ideas. Non-enclosed communities of sisters—those teaching in schools, managing hospitals, and working as home and foreign missioners—had begun a process of renewal that touched on the education and formation of sisters.[15] Pope Pius XII, who believed that a shortage of vocations could be tied to the tendency of sisters to "cling to antiquated customs," supported their efforts and welcomed requests "for any changes in constitution, rule, custom and ascetical practices that would modernize the spirit and works of the individual community."[16] Because the pope had seen the difficult position that monasteries were put into during the war—isolated from one another, unable to communicate and offer support where needed—he encouraged cloistered sisters to meet together to exchange ideas. In November 1950, the Vatican issued the apostolic constitution *Sponsa Christi*, which encouraged cloistered communities to form federations for the purpose of intra-community cooperation. Although the document reassured sisters that monasteries would retain their autonomy within the proposed federations, many contemplative communities hesitated to make this collaborative step.

Although hopes for a Carmelite federation had to be put on hold for nearly twenty years, the Indianapolis sisters attended a series of conferences on *Sponsa Christi* and related documents led by their chaplain, Father Raymond Bosler, in 1951. When he encouraged them to accept this challenge to adapt their lives, they were more enthusiastic than the sisters in many other Carmelite monasteries, who believed that the very idea of going out to meetings, even those encouraged by the pope, was counterintuitive to a cloistered life. Still, if part of the Carmelite spirit is openness to the future, adaptability, and an almost placid trust in divine providence—all manifest in the life and work of Teresa of Avila—then the Indianapolis community reflects that spirit. The sisters hosted the first meeting of Carmelite nuns gathered to discuss federation in 1954. The time was not fully ripe for change, but it would not be long. Vatican documents about adaptation to modern life and other ideas that eventually changed the concept of religious life—both cloistered and apostolic—began to take shape in religious communities in the 1950s, preparing sisters to be open to new ideas during and after the second Vatican council.

Meantime, life in the monastery went on much as it always had. The sisters helped to support themselves by making altar breads, vestments, and altar cloths, and with their calligraphy business. They kept the hours of the Divine Office, and balanced their lives of prayer between the demands of solitude and community interaction. When their families came to visit, they met them in rooms divided by grilles. When they attended Mass each day, they were separated from the congregation and not really visible, even to the priest. Although they were attuned to some events in the world and aware of some of the changes occurring in the church, they were primarily defined by enclosure, pursuing lives of solitary prayer apart from the world. If things were changing in those days leading up to Vatican II, it was not obvious in the daily practices inside the monastery. There, as in Teresa's time, one could see sisters such as those she saw in Saint Joseph's: "On account of Him who they know loves them, they close themselves up forever in a house without income, like someone who doesn't esteem her life. They give up everything; neither do they want their own will, nor does it even occur to them that they could be unhappy with such enclosure and austerity: together they all offer themselves as a sacrifice to God" (*Life* 39.10).

At the same time, winds of change were in the air. Teresa herself, though she hoped to live her remaining years in her first foundation, actually spent most of her life traveling and establishing new monasteries. If her own designs were dramatically changed, that was all right with her. She knew from years of experience that God's plans rarely conform to ours, and in the unique spiritual adventure she promised to her sisters—to be united in mutual love and a passion for God—she was open to the possibility of change. "I hold that love, where present, cannot possibly be content with remaining always the same," she told her sisters (*Castle*, Book VII, 4.9). She was talking about growing in the practice of the virtues, but her dynamism was soon to be experienced in much wider terms.

Notes

1 See Patricia Ranft, *Women and Religious Life in Premodern Europe* (New York: St. Martin's Press, 1998), chapters 1 through 6.

2 Elizabeth Makowski, *Canon Law and Cloistered Women* (Washington, D.C.: Catholic University of America Press, 1997), p. 28.

3 Peter F. Anson, "Papal Enclosure for Nuns," in *Cistercian Studies* (1968), pp. 109-23, 189-206.

4 Jodi Bilinkoff, *The Avila of Saint Teresa: Religious Reform in a Sixteenth-Century City* (Ithaca: Cornell University Press, 1989), p. 150.

5 Quoted in the introduction to *The Foundations*, translated and edited by Kieran Kavanaugh and Otilio Rodriguez (Washington, D.C.: Institute for Carmelite Studies Publications, 1985), p. 24.

6 Sections 15-20.

7 *Teresa of Avila* (Harrisburg, Pa.: Morehouse Publishing, 1991), p. 72. This book is a marvelous introduction to Teresa as she develops a model of Christian life as friendship with God.

8 These west wing cells were dedicated to the novitiate, and because Canon Law specified that a novitiate needed to be in its own separate space, the cells were set inside an additional corridor and set off by way of a wrought iron chain barrier. They are therefore smaller than the cells on the south side of the house.

9 In 1942 there was still no full bathroom in the "out quarters." The lavatory (with sink and toilet) that had been used by Miriam, Agnes, and Anne was still in place, but there was no tub or shower except within the enclosure. Until 1952, when a shower was installed in the guest bathroom, retreat directors either had rooms at Saint Vincent's Hospital or used the shower facilities in Mr. Zurschmied's cottage on the monastery property.

10 One of Mr. Marchetti's capitals was not installed, though no one remembers why. It is beautiful and elaborate and today is used decoratively in one of the small chapels inside the house.

11 Although they had a generous donation of funds for this statue in the late 1940s, the actual rendering of the statue took some time. An American sculptor turned down the opportunity but recommended a Dutch craftsman instead. When he submitted his model to the sisters, however, they found it unacceptable. Finally, they were led to a Dutch Augustinian sister, Monica van Seumeren, whose work they very much admired. A magazine section cover story in the Sunday *Indianapolis Star* (July 6, 1952) let people see what they otherwise could not have seen, since it was in place inside the cloister.

12 The monastery in Newport was in need of help and welcomed the presence of three seasoned Carmelites. Unfortunately, Mother Elizabeth died in Boston in 1944. When her sisters returned to Iceland in 1945, it was apparently almost as hard to get them back home as it had been to bring them over here.

13 Mother Agnes was accompanied by Sisters Joan, Mary, Magdalene, Catherine, Elia, and Patricia.

14 The Reno foundation was led by Mother Angela Macy, accompanied by Sisters Anne, Rose, Joseph, Marian, Mary Therese, Amie, and Elizabeth. Marian (Quinlan) eventually returned to Indianapolis.

15 See Mary Jo Weaver, *New Catholic Women* (1986; reprint, Bloomington: Indiana University Press, 1995), pp. 71-108.

16 See Sister Bertrande Meyers, *Sisters for the 21st Century* (New York: Sheed and Ward, 1965), p. 45.

5 Moving Stillness

This chapter considers prayer and change. The challenge to adapt to the needs of the modern world while remaining small, poor, and enclosed led the sisters to open their lives to others by sharing the Carmelite gift of contemplative prayer. I begin with prayer, a practice meant for everyone that became the basis for monastic life. I then describe how Teresa of Avila combined the primitive Rule about "prayer without ceasing" with her own daring innovations before I turn to the building of the final wing of the Indianapolis monastery in 1960 and the lives of the sisters up to the installation of the new doors in 1988. The sisters built their permanent chapel on the eve of Vatican II. The council's "universal call to holiness" changed the sisters and changed the way they related to the world. Like Teresa of Avila, they experienced God's dynamism, overriding their plans and opening them to a new future.

CHANGING OURSELVES

In mid-twentieth-century America, generations of Catholic schoolchildren were taught that prayer was "raising your minds and hearts to God," a definition distinguished by simplicity and grounded on a profound truth. However much prayer can be distorted into a way to manipulate divine providence, or dismissed as an essentially useless but interesting exercise in thought control, prayer is the way believers interact with God. Prayer "is a conscious, deliberate coming to terms with our actual situation before God."[1] In the preconciliar acronym, there were four ACTS of prayer: *adoration* recognized the sovereign majesty of God; *contrition* acknowledged our failings in the light of divine mercy; *thanksgiving* admitted our debts to God's goodness; and *supplication* allowed us to voice our own needs and those of others. These modes of prayer could be applied to the Mass or to devotions, to public prayer or to private conversation with God, but they were different from the prayer activity pursued in monasteries by monks and nuns. Their kind of constant prayer, said to require heroic dedication and withdrawal from the world, was thought to be out of reach for ordinary people living distracted lives.

In her reform movement, Teresa told her sisters that they were not doing anything new, since the primitive Rule was written to promote continual prayer. Closed away from the world in small communities, Teresa's sisters were told to "pray without ceasing." That injunction, however, found in Paul's first letter to the Thessalonians (5.17), was directed to *all* Christians, not simply to those in monastic life. Yet, although everyone was called to prayer and found some way to practice it, a life dedicated to prayer was connected to the

OPPOSITE: CIRCULAR STAIRCASE FROM NORTH CORRIDOR TO LOWER LEVEL
PREVIOUS SPREAD: AERIAL VIEW OF COMPLETED MONASTERY, 1961

monastic movement. There, supported by the "counsels of perfection," prayer could be a full-time occupation and find a number of different expressions. In medieval monasteries, monks and nuns talked about three kinds of prayer: oral (saying the Divine Office, for example), meditative (reflecting on the divine mysteries by using Scripture), and contemplative, the highest of all forms because it had no concrete object, and because it was a direct, unmediated connection between God and the soul, a mystical encounter.

The history of Western spirituality has many methods to help one still the memory, will, and intellect in order to be in a position to receive God's gift of mystical union. While monks and nuns could seek contemplative union, they could not achieve it, a situation that led practitioners to speculate about the mechanics and parameters of contemplation and mystical union. In the early years of the twentieth century, Harvard psychologist William James read through mountains of literature on this subject and concluded that mystical experience—the apex of contemplation—has four characteristics: it is passive (it happens to a person and is therefore beyond his or her control), transient (it cannot be sustained), noetic (one who has had a mystical experience knows something), and ineffable (it is beyond human comprehension and description).[2]

The fact that mysticism cannot be described has, paradoxically, only stimulated the desire to explain it. In broad terms, spiritual writers have described two basic methods: one involves or moves through discourse and images (kataphatic), and the other is drawn away from words and images, moving into a deeper presence (apophatic).[3] These paths toward mystical prayer either work with or try to empty the contents of consciousness. The first is rooted in the belief that human beings need images and concepts to connect with God; the second aims to empty consciousness in order to make room for the divine. Great spiritual teachers or mystics usually experience both, though they may later emphasize one of them. Why some people are drawn to one or another way may be a facet of personality: both ways can be found in world religions; both have long histories behind them and effective methods within them. Neither of them can fully explain the mysterious experience of contemplative union. Age-old questions continue to be asked about whether one can train oneself for it, whether the path of contemplation is open to everyone or to a select few, and what metaphor best describes the experience.

Carmelite spirituality as found in the experience and writings of Teresa of Avila and John of the Cross is a consciousness-emptying attentiveness in which a self-lavishing God makes space within us and fills it.[4] Teresa entered a monastery where the sisters said the Divine Office and were expected to engage in a certain style of vocal prayer, often for patrons of the house. Her middle-aged conversion experience, described in her *Life*, led her to a new conception of prayer as companionship with Christ, and began a life-long practice of surrender. Once she was really able to say "thy will be done," she found God's will being done in and through her, changing her plans and transforming her life. Put another way, she discovered the key to prayer: it does not change God, it changes us.

THE PARADOX OF TERESA'S EXPERIENCE OF PRAYER

Teresa entered the monastery of the Incarnation because she thought its Rule was one she could keep. Like many other people of her time, she had neither heard about nor been encouraged to practice mental prayer. Like many women around her, she was schooled in deference to ecclesiastical and political officials, not to self-confidence. And as a descendant of a *converso*, she had reason to be fearful of the Inquisition, with its obsessions about blood purity. Her plans included life in an austere but comfortable monastery where prescribed hours of prayer would be punctuated by family visits and witty interactions with important visitors. It was not to be. As a young sister, so ill that she could not be cared for in the monastery, she was sent home and then to a healer. In the middle of this mysterious illness, which took some years to disappear, she was introduced to a new kind of prayer through reading Francisco de Osuna's *The Third Spiritual Alphabet*.[5]

Osuna and other Franciscans, along with Jesuits and other reformers, were increasingly suspicious of externals and confident about the possibility of inner transformation. They recommended "recollection," a method to simplify prayer and draw the soul away from distractions so that it could be opened to God's action at its deepest level. In the eyes of the Inquisition, this new mode of prayer—indeed, all personal, silent prayer—was dangerous because it suggested that it was possible to make contact with God directly rather than through the ways mediated by the church. Teresa, however, was not only drawn to this kind of prayer, she increasingly felt as if God ordered her to do it. Her early experiences with God's presence in her life frightened her, as well they might in a culture that found such encounters diabolical or delusional. In her *Life*, she repeatedly explains how and why she sought the advice of confessors and other learned men to help her explain her own experience. She knew, as did everyone else, that people practicing private prayer, especially women, were considered dangerous and deranged. Yet she persisted, fighting through years of agonizing self-doubt and the knowing judgment of "learned men" that, indeed, she was being deceived by the devil.

Teresa spent the first forty years of her life aware of her inner fragmentation. She desired God, but feared that desire. Put another way, she wanted to surrender but did not know how. When her controlled attempts to abandon herself to God went nowhere, God relinquished Himself to her in a profoundly simple way. One day, when she was tired and in the chapel, she looked at an image of the wounded Christ that she may have looked at hundreds of times before but not really seen. This time she saw it: Christ alone, afflicted, and in need of her. In His weakened condition, Christ had to accept her. And in this moment, recounted in chapter 9 of her *Life*, all her desires to be needed, all the contrivances to please people that had marked her life up to then, melted in the certainty of being loved and wanted by Christ in His agony. In this moment, she experienced prayer as friendship with Christ, a politically dangerous concept, but overwhelming and empowering for her and the source of all her later self-confidence. Her reform movement would be based on that certainty and would combine this daring new form of prayer with a highly traditional form of life in a small, enclosed monastery.

Teresa was never an organized writer and was not one for consistent definitions, but she understood what it meant to be a contemplative. It "was essentially a matter of the sustained awareness of living within the movement of God's love into creation through the life and death of Jesus Christ."[6] Prayer for her was companionship with the suffering Jesus, and the reformed communities she founded were established on that principle. A small community was, for her, an expression of friendship with Christ, in which members can meet whatever life brings their way because they make themselves available to the "man of sorrows," who, in turn, is their most compassionate witness. As Teresa understood it, God is looking not for admirers but for helpers, and prayer begins with a desire to stick with it, which was her way of embracing the cross. Those who manage this first step—deceptively simple yet frustratingly difficult—find that prayer will disclose its secrets: prayer is not about saving our souls, but involves remaining with Christ across time and space, entering the cosmic adventure that is eternally present in the death and resurrection of Christ. In this way Christ is always present, always in need of friendship so that His friends may be transformed into companions of a suffering world. Prayer, then, is deep conversation with Christ, and "the discovery of the self in and through conversation with Christ is a discovery of the kinship with God bestowed by grace [which is] a discovery of an ever-expanding space of human growth in love and understanding."[7]

One of Teresa's most salient characteristics was courage. She was a visionary whose experience led her into contemplative prayer and cloistered life even as it opened her to explore new territories. She succeeded in an impossible task, reforming an existing monastic tradition as a woman of Jewish descent in late medieval Spain. She managed to translate her own experience of prayer into terms that her sisters could practice, telling them that "the Lord invites all" (*Way* 19.15) to the adventure of contemplative prayer and mystical union. The wit that distinguished her younger life and made her a much-sought-after companion was now transferred to her reform movement, where her mixture of determination and humor invested her sisters with a sense of mission. She explained prayer as being present to the Presence within oneself and urged her sisters to seek God in themselves in every possible circumstance. "Don't be sad, daughters, when obedience draws you to involvement in exterior matters. Know that if it is in the kitchen, the Lord walks among the pots and pans helping you both interiorly and exteriorly" (*Foundations* 5.8). The life she designed for her sisters was austere, but rooted in joy. She wanted her sisters to know the bliss that comes from "throwing ourselves into the arms of this Lord of ours" (*Meditation on the Song of Songs* 5.8).

Above all, a community based on Teresa's experience had to be prepared for interruptions. Striving to be what God wants means a willingness to relinquish one's own plans. In personal terms, such occasions occur regularly, and sisters were expected to sacrifice personal comfort and desire for the good of the community. In collective terms, the pattern of interruption that Teresa experienced from God in her life might mean openness to newness and fearlessness in the face of challenge. The Carmelite community of Indianapolis, true to her legacy, has that personality. From Emma Seelbach to the present, its leadership has often been in the hands of pioneers with adventuresome spirits and confidence in God.

THE NEW CHAPEL AND OTHER CHANGES IN INDIANAPOLIS

1960 was an auspicious year for the Indianapolis community. In July, construction began on the final wing of the building, featuring a new choir (where the sisters gathered for community prayer) and the much-anticipated but modestly rendered new chapel (where members of the public gathered for daily liturgy).[8] A main altar surrounded by exquisitely tall wooden doors and grilles separated these two places of worship. During Mass, the doors were opened so that the sisters could hear the service, though they could neither see nor be seen by the public. Along with the choir and chapel, the sisters designed a new recreation room, an infirmary, and new workrooms. A graceful curved stairway to the lower level was erected in the corridor between the choir and the court, and the upstairs level was remodeled so that the sisters could finally get from one place to another on the upper floor with-

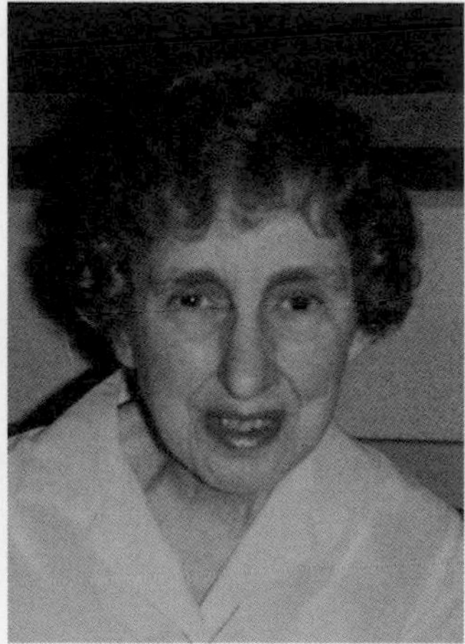

THREE PHOTOS OF MIRIAM ELDER: FULL HABIT (1967), MODIFIED HABIT (1972), LAY CLOTHES (1983)

THE CHOIR, C. 1961

out having to go downstairs. What had been the Little Flower Chapel was now a connecting hallway, and the statue of the Little Flower from that shrine was moved to the south end of the front hallway, where the public could still see it. The large workroom on the west side of the outer quarters was redesigned to become three rooms: a permanent visiting room with a latticed grille, a bathroom for visitors on the public side, and a flower room on the cloister side. The bells that had been purchased in anticipation of the large church two decades earlier were now installed above the new choir. In late July 1961, construction was finished and the new wing opened to visitors. An elaborate photo essay appeared in the *Indianapolis Star*. The chapel, where the public could attend daily Mass on their side of the separating grille while the sisters attended in their choir, was dedicated in August.

As these events were occurring in the monastery, bishops all over the world were anticipating the opening of an ecumenical council, announced by Pope John XXIII in 1959. The country was under the leadership of its first Roman Catholic president, and a variety of movements (against the war, for women's rights and civil rights) and new ini-

SISTER AT COMMUNION WINDOW, C.1961

BEGINNINGS OF DIALOGUE AFTER VATICAN II, 1968

tiatives (the Peace Corps) had fired the passions of many Americans. Although the sisters were becoming increasingly aware of events in the national and world news, they were mostly focused on the coming council. Their former chaplain and editor of the diocesan newspaper, Father Raymond Bosler, would accompany Archbishop Schulte to the council as his theological expert (*peritus*). Father Bosler was, accordingly, in an excellent position to guide the sisters through the documents of Vatican II, though the sisters were in many ways ready for the council. For example, even though nothing had come of it at the time, they had hosted the first meeting to discuss a Carmelite federation in 1954 and were eager to pursue that option. Distinguished scholars such as John L. McKenzie (Scripture) and Louis Bouyer (Liturgy), whose work would help to guide Catholics in the post-conciliar church, had visited the monastery and given talks there. The new "dialogue Mass" was begun at the monastery in 1959.

The 1960s were a decade of firsts for the sisters. They used an organ for liturgy for the first time in 1963, and like people in parishes, they began to do some of the readings at Mass and anticipated the English liturgy. They began saying the Divine Office in English in December 1964 and experimenting with a new daily schedule in 1965. When Pope Paul VI addressed the United Nations in October 1965, the sisters watched television for the first time. In 1967 they had their first dialogue homily, and hoped to become a center for liturgical experimentation. These were years of expanding horizons for the sisters: they

CHOIR MODIFIED TO SUIT POST–VATICAN II LITURGY, C. 1970

took courses on art appreciation and world religions offered in the monastery by faculty members at nearby Marian College.

As the sisters modified their lives to reflect the spirit of the council, they also sought ways to deepen their traditional vocation to prayer and solitude. They built new hermitages inside the monastery, and in July 1965 they experimented with a new form of solitude, a "hermit day" that suspended the normal schedule so that, apart from Mass, each sister could spend the day entirely apart from the community. In their discussion of the council documents, especially those related to religious life, they again began to discuss a Carmelite federation. For a number of reasons, early efforts to form a federation were not successful. In 1965, however, with support from Vatican officials, nuns from fifty-four Carmelite monasteries met in St. Louis to discuss various matters, including formation. This meeting was significant for two reasons: first, Carmelite authorities in Rome had not issued any instruction for the formation of nuns since the time of Teresa of Avila; and second, the sisters themselves had proposed the agenda and gave the papers there.

Although the meeting in St. Louis had some negative results—dividing Carmelites into those groups who wanted federation and those who did not, for example—it also stimulated some new initiatives and built a stronger sense of community and cohesiveness among many Carmelite sisters. The battle between women's religious orders and their male superiors was a leitmotif of female religious life in the years following the council. Nuns had

been examining and updating their lives for a decade before the council, and they were often more eager for change than were their male superiors in Rome. And, as I have shown elsewhere, many of them were eager to embrace the ideas of the women's movement.[9] Cloistered nuns were not as quick to embrace feminism, but as they encountered opposition to their desires to regulate their own lives or to be permitted to modify their own rules, they, too, pushed for more autonomy and self-direction.

One creative response to the St. Louis meeting in 1965 was the founding of the journal *Encounter* by the Carmelite monastery in Reno, Nevada. When those sisters showed other Carmelites a "sample issue," the sisters in St. Louis voted to establish the journal. Its first editor was Sister Teresa (Joan Williams) of the Carmelite monastery in Indianapolis. This inter-monastery quarterly of the Discalced Carmelites in the United States was meant to foster dialogue among the Carmelite sisters on a number of sensitive issues. It solicited reactions to the St. Louis meeting, opened for discussion the new "norms" and the new "constitution" issued for nuns by the Carmelite General in Rome, and encouraged sisters to be involved in the future direction of their lives. The diversity of Carmelite hopes for the future is obvious in the pages of the journal. Just as obvious is the increasing desire of the Indianapolis Carmel to be more in tune with a dynamic concept of cloister, more willing to share contemplative prayer with the laity, and less willing to be perceived as women in flight from the world.

A NEW UNDERSTANDING OF CONTEMPLATIVE LIFE

When Vatican II issued a "universal call to holiness," it challenged all Catholics to deepen their prayer lives. Those groups who had dedicated themselves to lives of prayer were challenged to express the essence of their charism in ways that fit the new consciousness of faith rooted in history and based on experience. In an article reprinted in *Encounter*, Gabriel Tilimans, a Dutch Carmelite priest, called for a "dynamic concept of cloister." A renewed theology of contemplation no longer considers enclosure as a flight from the world or a system designed to protect women, he argued, but "rather as a necessary disposition for this kind of life."[10] Cloister enables a particular form of Christian witness, one that immerses Carmelites in the dialectical process of turning toward the world to gather information and then separating from the world in order to contemplate the deeper mystery embedded in it. In this way, a contemplative community could realize its spiritual vocation in the actual life of the church. In addition, many contemplatives saw the need to serve the world by sharing faith and prayer with those who sought a deeper experience of God.

The sisters in Indianapolis moved steadily toward a new understanding of their contemplative life and the ways in which it could be made more visible and available to the needs of the world. In the late 1960s, the sisters began to remove barriers between themselves and the world even as they maintained a cloistered existence marked by solitary prayer. They removed the grilles and grates in their visiting rooms first (1967), then in the choir (1969). They began to go out of the monastery for dental appointments, to vote, and to meetings. In 1970, they were allowed to go home for visits for the first time since they had entered the monastery. Some went out to take courses or attend lectures. At the same time, sisters from non-cloistered communities came for visits in order to learn more about contemplative prayer. As they interacted more directly with people from outside the monastery, the sisters modified their habits and returned to their baptismal names. They experimented with a new process of accepting recruits, a three-month "live in," in which candidates who hoped to become members could participate fully in the daily life of the community.

As they discussed and modified their lives, the sisters also experimented with new work. Although changes in the fasting laws in the late 1950s had stimulated more reception of communion, increasing their altar bread business, the sisters were also looking for other income-producing activity. In 1977 they were introduced to the typesetting business, investigated its possibilities, and voted to buy a copywriter computer. When it arrived in the spring of 1978, the old vestment department was refitted for this new endeavor, and the sisters embarked on a business that would involve them in the production of some of the best examples of post-conciliar thinking being written. When personal computers made it possible for publishers to get their books typeset more economically than was possible with the copywriter computer, the sisters had to reconsider their options. They clearly needed an income-producing project to supplement the altar bread department, but it was not totally clear what would happen. Then, in one of those serendipitous conjunctions of events, they were able to turn a small project of their own into a major business. In their daily community prayer, they had been using an inclusive-language version of the Psalms, a booklet they had typeset with their equipment. Around 1983, they put these together for their own use in a small booklet, called *A Companion to the Breviary*. As people asked for copies, they published a second edition and began to sell it. In 1984 they published a

SISTER WORKING AT COMPUGRAPHIC EDIT WRITER, 1978

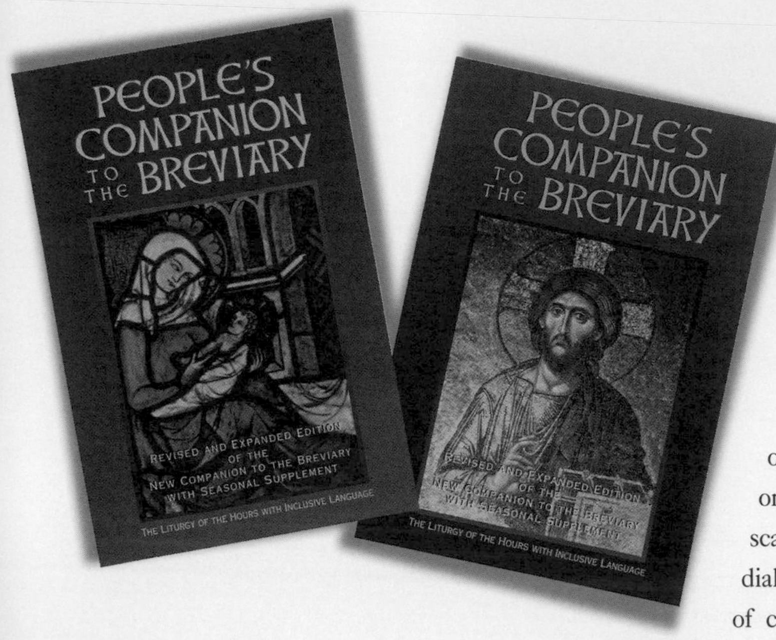

Seasonal Supplement, which included prayers and intercessions, followed by an additional book with Scriptural readings. Eventually, learning from each edition, they published the two-volume *People's Companion to the Breviary: The Liturgy of the Hours with Inclusive Language*, a project that has sold well over 100,000 copies worldwide.[11]

These changes in daily life were not the only events of those years. Two attempts to organize contemplative women on a national scale pushed the sisters into an ongoing dialectic about their lives and a new theology of contemplation. The Carmelite Communities Associated (CCA) was the fruit of those early conversations about federation, the St. Louis meeting, and the conviction on the part of the sisters that they needed to interact with one another in order to support a renewed sense of contemplative life. The Association of Contemplative Sisters (ACS) was founded in 1969 as a way for sisters from a variety of contemplative communities to meet regularly for mutual support and understanding. Both groups called for creative involvement as sisters tried to balance new ideas, traditional understandings of their lives, perceived needs to have some control of their own lives, and the desire of lay people to share the life of contemplative prayer.

ACS sponsored six-week educational forums for four successive years in the 1970s. It stimulated feminist discussion within contemplative communities that were trying to renew themselves according to the documents of Vatican II and to gain some control over their own lives. ACS welcomed lay women contemplatives first as "friends," then as "associates," and in 1986 as full members, becoming a place for Catholic women who were following a contemplative path in their own lives. By the mid-1990s, the membership in ACS was predominantly lay women, but many sisters still attend meetings, including sisters from the Indianapolis monastery, who from the beginning have been important supporters, elected officers, and enthusiastic members of this group.

OPEN TO THE FUTURE

Carmelite sisters founded by the reforming efforts of Teresa of Avila were energized by her spirit and responsive to the needs of their time. In the sixteenth century, in the context of religious wars, the Protestant reformation, and political instability, Teresa saw that the best way to serve God was in the context of a rigorously enclosed, selectively small, unendowed monastic movement. Her Rule was based on the earliest Carmelite legislation, and thus was, in its way, highly traditional. At the same time, her form of prayer was rooted in her experience of God fully present within the deepest center of her own soul, and was completely daring in its day. Her confidence in God gave her the courage to do something new in a time when new ideas could lead one into the arms of the Inquisition. However much she longed for peace and quiet, she was committed to a God who continually interrupted her plans and inspired her to move into uncharted territories. When the second Vatican council asked sisters to return to the original charism and spirit of their founders, it opened the door for some Carmelites to find that original charism in their founder's daring openness to the future. The sisters in Indianapolis have been shaped by that courage.

Notes

1 Richard McBrien, *Catholicism* (Minneapolis: Winston Press, 1980), p. 332.

2 *The Varieties of Religious Experience* (1902; reprint, New York: New American Library, 1958), p. 328.

3 See Willigis Jäger, *Search for the Meaning of Life: Essays and Reflections on the Mystical Experience* (Liguori, Mo.: Triumph Books, 1989), pp. 81-95.

4 Iain Matthew, *The Impact of God* (London: Hodder and Stoughton, 1995), is a brilliant and accessible introduction to John of the Cross, the systematic theological genius of the Carmelite reform movement.

5 First published in 1527, this book by a Franciscan friar recommended "recollection" to women and lay people, which drew the suspicion of the Inquisition. See Mary E. Giles, ed., *Francisco De Osuna: The Third Spiritual Alphabet* (New York: Paulist Press, 1982).

6 Rowan Williams, *Teresa of Avila* (Harrisburg, Pa.: Morehouse Publishing, 1991), p. 10.

7 Ibid., p. 92.

8 The first wing of the monastery was built (1932) after the foundation for the entire building had been poured. The sisters at that time intended to build a very large chapel with a crypt and a magnificent upper church with an altar surrounded by a large grille separating the choir from the church. By the time the last wing was built (1960), however, the plans had changed, so that the new chapel would be considerably more modest. At the same time, the builders had to work with what they had, viz., a lower floor (originally intended to be the crypt) and an upper one. They decided to make the entrance (lower) level into the public chapel and to situate the sisters in the choir on the upper level. At that time, the sisters were still separated from the public in all things, including worship.

9 See my *New Catholic Women* (1986; reprint, Bloomington: Indiana University Press, 1995), chapter 3.

10 Originally published in *Tijdsschrift voor geestelijk Leven* in 1967, this article was revised and published in the intra-Carmelite journal published at the Carmelite monastery in Indianapolis. See *Encounter*, vol. III, no. 2 (1968), pp. 22-31.

11 This two-volume set, copyright 1997, includes a revised and expanded edition of the *New Companion* along with the *Seasonal Supplement*. In other words, this final product contains not only the Psalms, but Scripture readings, intercessions, and feast day celebrations with particular attention to saintly women. For a complete list of the books published by the Indianapolis Carmel, see their Web site, www.praythenews.com.

6 A Door to the Universe

This chapter focuses on spirituality, specifically a new spiritual consciousness rooted in tradition and given new form in the second Vatican council. The "universal call to holiness" recognizes that Christ called everyone to perfection. I begin with a selective outline of Christian spirituality as a specific response to God's invitation to relationship, paying particular attention to the insight of Pierre Teilhard de Chardin that a God who shines through the universe wants to be found in all things. I then use some of the ideas of Teresa of Avila and John of the Cross to show how the sisters in the Indianapolis Carmel have responded to the challenge to be more present to the world. The architectural feature of this chapter—the installation in 1988 of the new doors between the choir and chapel—opens out to www.praythenews.com, the Web site the sisters developed in 2001 to share their spirituality with the world.

CHRISTIAN SPIRITUALITY

Scripture is alive with the nearness and presence of God and the invitation to respond to divine initiative by way of the commands to love God and love one's neighbor. Christian spirituality took shape in the teachings and events in the life of Jesus and the attempts of the earliest communities to articulate their understanding of Christ's life as a moment of new creation for them. Believers received the Holy Spirit in baptism, were nurtured by the community (its celebration and remembrance of Jesus), and were urged to live as saints, since God was now alive in them through Christ. They were to be dead to sin and to seek a more human, loving way of life rooted in imitation of Christ. Christian spirituality involved conversion (shedding the old self), expectation (that Christ would soon return for them), and mission (to proclaim the good news of this new life to the world). Imitation of Christ meant praying without ceasing in order to seek God's will and express God's love for the world by way of service, but that vocation was continually shaped by historical circumstances.

In times of persecution, martyrdom offered an especially clear pathway to the imitation of Christ. When the persecutions ceased and the Christian church took on some of the political characteristics of the empire, flight to the desert in search of a hermitage and an ascetical life became the new ideal of Christian spirituality. There one could pray without ceasing and seek God wholeheartedly, but only by rejecting the world. As monastic life grew into a system, it developed an accompanying theology that raised some questions that monks and nuns continue to refine. Was the purpose of spiritual life the rejec-

OPPOSITE: NEW DOORS BETWEEN CHOIR AND CHAPEL, 1988
PREVIOUS SPREAD: SISTERS IN LOWER CHAPEL, 2001

tion of all earthly understanding in order to be absolutely absorbed in the knowledge of God?[1] Or was it geared toward self-knowledge in the light of Christ? Augustine, who moved spirituality in this more psychological direction, also raised an enduring spiritual paradox: no one, he said, should be so immersed in contemplation as to ignore the needs of his or her neighbor, and no one should be so absorbed in action as to dispense with the contemplation of God.[2]

As monasticism developed, so did ascetical practices based on the so-called "counsels of perfection" (poverty, chastity, and obedience). Spirituality in this setting was practical: the Rule of Saint Benedict, for example, was designed to balance a life of prayer and work. In the twelfth century, however, the practical spirituality of monastic life took a mystical turn in the writings of Bernard of Clairvaux (1090-1153), whose reflections on Scripture led to his belief that God's love is self-revealing. For Bernard, as for later mystics, God's love for humanity is expressed in longing and searching: God seeks us and wants to be sought by us. When Bernard reflected on Scripture, as all monks did, he saw an outpouring of divine goodness. For him, love is the only object of the sacred texts whose history is, in reality, our history.[3] Contemplative knowledge thus has two objects, self-understanding (searching self-judgment) and faith in God's kindness rooted in desire (the form that love takes in our earthly existence). Later, in fourteenth-century England, Julian of Norwich echoed Bernard's sense that God is present in human desire, and that where God is concerned, seeking is as good as finding. Hers is a mystical theology of love and gentleness. "God always wants us to be secure in love," she says, "and peaceful and restful, as he is towards us."[4]

Because spirituality is dynamic, it is constantly reaffirming its priorities. The imitation of Christ reflects the circumstances in which one is trying to achieve it. In mendicant orders such as the Franciscans and the Dominicans, Christian spirituality found a way to emphasize radical poverty and mission, rooting spirituality in action. Yet fourteenth-century Rhineland mystics such as Meister Eckhart returned to the highly detached spirituality of Dionysius the Areopagite. How was Christian spirituality best expressed? Thomas Aquinas (c. 1225-74) suggested sharing with others what had been contemplated. Ignatius of Loyola (1491-1556), who was described by a friend as "contemplation in action,"[5] based Jesuit spirituality on a unity of prayer and action in the world, a system particularly responsive to the needs of the post-Reformation church. In that same spirit, Francis de Sales (d. 1622) and others sought to free spirituality from its monastic expression and bring it into the lives of all Christians by focusing on the joy of Christian existence. Adoration, communion, and cooperation expressed a seventeenth-century French spirituality that was similar to the early Christian community: one imitated Christ by looking upon Jesus, uniting oneself to Christ, and then acting lovingly in the world.

CONTEMPORARY SPIRITUALITY AND VATICAN II

As Catholic spirituality moved into the modern world, the questions raised throughout its history were addressed in terms of holiness and prayer. Could one balance contemplation and action, or must one choose between them? Was the spiritual life meant only for monks and nuns, or for everyone? Was holiness a matter of self-knowledge before God in the midst of a busy life, or a withdrawal from the world in order to seek God absolutely? Was it possible to become a mystic while in the world? Perhaps the most creative modern response to these questions was that of French Jesuit paleontologist Pierre Teilhard de Chardin (1881-1955).

In the middle years of the twentieth century, Teilhard developed a spirituality oriented to the world, based on his understanding of divine presence in matter and in the evolving universe. Although not appreciated in his time—and, in fact, silenced by his superiors—his work has been foundational for contemporary creation-centered spirituality. In the midst of the First World War, when he worked as a chaplain, he experienced the fundamental oneness of the universe: "creation has never stopped," he wrote; "the creative act is one huge continual gesture drawn out over the totality of time. It is still going on."[6] Unlike Bernard, who saw God's loving divulgence primarily in Scripture, Teilhard was fascinated with the entire universe as "a divine milieu," in which God was actively self-disclosing. The more Teilhard learned about the world, the closer God was to him. He was a mystic of a new kind, whose experience of God was not based on an ascetical practice apart from the world, but grew out of his belief that one encounters God by turning to the things of the earth. There, in the natural delight one takes in life—and in all that has existed from the first moment of creation—one finds the divine, longing to be seen and loved. "The great mystery of Christianity is not that God appears (epiphany) but that God shines through the universe (diaphany). Our prayer, therefore, is not that we might see God 'as He is in Himself' but that we might see God in all things."[7]

Teilhard's spiritual masterpiece, *The Divine Milieu*, was begun in 1926, precisely because he was unsatisfied with traditional ways of posing the questions of holiness. He came up "with a twofold answer that provided him with the structure for his book: 'the divinization of activities' and 'the divinization of passivities' represent a continuous process of transformation whereby we can find communion with God in the world."[8] Mysticism for him was a collective journey in tune with the universe. "It is impossible to love Christ without loving others," he wrote, "and it is impossible to love others (in a spirit of broad human communion) without moving nearer to Christ."[9] Teilhard's spirituality, though written before the council, was not readily available until afterward. Today it is at the heart of a dynamic new spirituality. In the middle years of the twentieth century, however, it was not very influential.

On the contrary, modern challenges of secularism and scientific discovery tended to make Christian spirituality individualistic and defensive even as new theological currents in Scripture, liturgy, and historical studies created the atmosphere that would eventually lead to Vatican II. At the council, the rigid spirituality that focused on external expressions and a highly individualized prayer life were replaced by a return to a biblically based spirituality of personal conversion and witness. Christian spirituality was to be grounded in Scripture and to begin with human experience. The mystery of the Trinity and the centrality of Christ were emphasized in a theology that was rooted in a concept of union with Christ in the mystical body of the church. Most important, the council addressed the whole church, including the laity, in its universal call to holiness.

Lumen Gentium, the dogmatic constitution on the church issued by the second Vatican council in 1964, devotes a chapter to the "call to holiness."[10] It states that Jesus called everyone to the holiness and perfection possible through a profound love for God and neighbor. Although holiness is an attribute of God, it was made visible in a special way in Christ and is accessible to Christians through their reception of the Holy Spirit in baptism. All are encouraged to liberate themselves from everything that hinders love so that they can participate in the mission of the church, which is the sanctification of the world. Holiness, therefore, seeks ways to express and carry out that charge wherever one is. If the council makes clear that all Christians are to cultivate one and the same holiness, it also recognizes a variety of approaches to it. Different modes of spirituality, especially when in communication with one another, strengthen the human journey toward God. Monastic life is a particularly intense, counter-cultural response to the universal call to holiness, a consecration to God that signifies a lifelong commitment to seek God in prayer so as to find God in the unpredictability of life.

WORLD-EMBRACING SPIRITUALITY AND THE CARMELITE TRADITION

In his book *Cosmology and Creation*, contemporary philosopher Paul Brockelman begins with observations of astronauts that the planets manifest the divine and that the universe is awe-inspiring. Like Teilhard, he sees creation as a continual process with transformative possibilities. When he laments the inability of alienated modern people to find a sense of wonder from the universe, he suggests, paradoxically, that science (not religion) can open their eyes. "I believe that our religious traditions and indeed the spiritual life of all humankind emerge out of this jaw-dropping experience of wonder that strikes the human mind as it experiences the inexplicable grandeur of all creation."[11] The "Big Bang," the new creation story, is how science explains ultimate reality breaking into ordinary space and time to connect us with a deeper existence to which all belong. Modern science, precisely because it realizes that it cannot know everything, can make mystics of all of us, since it teaches what contemplatives have always known: that reality is emergent, novel, unpredictable, creative, and expanding.

Like those who espouse a creation-centered spirituality inspired by Teilhard, Brockelman believes that ultimate reality comprises everything: nature, humanity, the cosmos, and the divine form a unity, however multiform it might be. All life, therefore, is holy in its fascinating diversity. Cosmologists Thomas Berry and Brian Swimme are drawn precisely to the infinite diversity of the universe:

> What is particularly striking is the lack of repetition in the developing universe. The fireball that begins the universe gives way to the galactic emergence and the first generation of stars. The later generations of stars bring into being the living planets with their own sequence of epochs, each differentiating itself from the rest. Biological and human history with their ever-fresh expressions of creativity continue the differentiation of time from its beginning. Indeed all fifteen billion years form an epic that must be viewed as a whole to understand its full meaning. This meaning is the extravagance of the creative outpouring, where each being is given its unique existence. At the heart of the universe is an outrageous bias for the novel, for the unfurling of surprise in prodigious dimensions throughout the vast range of existence.[12]

What if the universal call to holiness were translated into these cosmic terms so that one approached the universe with the same desires one had in pursuing a spiritual path? What would it mean to seek God's will in perfect charity in relation to creation? Could the diversity of the cosmos itself invite a variety of spiritual pathways?

It is not as improbable as it might seem to connect hymns to the universe with the spirituality of Teresa of Avila and John of the Cross. They were both convinced that God is hidden in the depths of one's soul, and that each person should seek union with the divine in solitude and silence. One possible application of Carmelite spirituality to cosmology might be to think of God's intimate presence in the depths of the universe. The divine is hidden in the world, waiting there, as in the individual soul, to be discovered, surrendered to, and trusted. If God dwells in the present historical experience, it is conceivable that one could find passionate union with the divine in the soul of the universe. Paradoxically, a life apart from the world may have a special affinity for this quest. Solitude, contemplation, efforts to establish a community of mutual care, and the desire to find, adore, and love God in oneself—all part of traditional Carmelite life—can be adapted to a cosmological perspective. In the process, the cloister is not an Eden set apart from the world, but a school of contemplation within the world. Since contemplatives experience God as one who works in darkness, they can turn toward the world with an attentive, resilient, loving gaze.

John obviously thought about the relationship between the created order and the divine. *The Spiritual Canticle* acknowledges the power of the created order to enkindle a desire for God. His most dramatic statement, however, can be found in a little-known set of poems, romances on the Gospel. In these nine ballads of the Incarnation, he took pains to describe the internal life of the Trinitarian God, and to explain why God created the world and then entered into it as a human being. He began by evoking the infinite happiness of the Trinity, where Father, Son, and Holy Spirit are so unified in boundless love that they are, in fact, one lover and one beloved. Although totally contented, the Father tells the Son that He wishes to give him a "bride who will love you. Because of you she will deserve to share our company." The Son is overjoyed by this suggestion because he knows that in showing his brightness to this bride, she will "see how great my Father is, and how I have received my being from your being. I will hold her in my arms, and she will burn with your love, and with eternal delight. She will exalt in your goodness." The Father then said, "let it be done, for your love has deserved it, and by these words, the world was created."

These ballads contain two startling ideas. First, the bride herself is not the church or the Virgin Mary, but the entire universe, heaven and earth, angels and human beings. Second, at the scene of Christ's birth, angels and human beings burst into celebratory song at the "marriage of two such as these" (divinity and the universe), but "God there in the manger cried and moaned." The incarnate God has a love so self-emptying and vulnerable that the birth of Jesus brings joy to humanity even as God learns to cry. "In God, man's weeping, and in man, gladness, to the one and the other, things usually so strange."[13]

FAITH SHARING, 1982

If God is at the center of the cosmos, and if contemplative spirituality is engaged in a desire to find God and to ponder the divine mysteries, then Carmelites can open themselves to the mystical embrace of the world. The Carmelite acceptance of darkness as a venue of divine disclosure, and the universal call to holiness and the dynamic approach to cloister that began to take shape in the years following the council together form a new pattern that can deepen the old one. Contemplatives turn toward the

LITURGY OF THE HOURS, 2001

world to gather information and then withdraw from it in order to probe its deeper mysteries, to seek union with ultimate Mystery as it constantly pours itself into the universe. If the world needs wisdom, then perhaps the insights that can be gained through a life of contemplation can help those who seek to connect ordinary life to the sacred.

NEW DOORS AND PRAYTHENEWS.COM

In 1985, one of the sisters received a substantial legacy from a deceased aunt, who had specified that it be spent on a "work of art." That gift came at a time when the sisters had decided to renovate the choir in order to make their liturgical space more adaptable to the directives of the second Vatican council. They needed to replace the old cork floor, to give the place a fresh look, and to buy new chairs. They also decided to remove the old altar and to commission a new one. The legacy enabled these changes and allowed the sisters to make a dramatic artistic statement by replacing the old fourteen-foot-high wooden door separating the choir from the chapel. In September 1987, rigging was moved into the choir to remove the old marble altar and the large wooden doors surrounding it.[14] In subsequent months the choir was painted, a new parquet floor was laid down, and new furniture was moved in. At the end of February 1988, the new doors were installed.

Ken vonRoenn, who designed the doors, is a Kentucky artist whose work had attracted the attention of one of the sisters. When he came to the monastery in October 1987, he brought some slides of his work, including some photographs of a set of windows that evoked moving water. As he met with the sisters to hear their ideas and talk about their life, the importance of water and movement held his attention. He returned in November with two designs, and the sisters chose the more abstract of the two. When he later wrote his own reflection on the design, he said that he had been influenced by the importance of water in the work of Teresa of Avila[15] and "the concept of life as an evolutionary resurrection towards the spiritual union with God, the source of all life."[16] His design used several shapes and colors: circular forms, beveled glass arcs, reflective mirrors, streaky blue glass, and white painted glass were meant to evoke the unity of God, an animated, dynamic universal order, the spiritual nature of water, and the purity of spiritual existence. The abstract design of the doors invites viewers to find their own meaning in them, but whatever that might be, the doors reflect the changing light of the seasons and draw the viewer into their color, size, and energy.

SISTER IN READING ROOM, 2001

Dynamism expressed in a work of art is one thing. When experienced in daily life, it challenges one to adapt. As the sisters looked toward the future in the late 1990s, hopeful that their way of life would attract new people and continue, they realized that they had to revise their ideas about formation and mission. As they anticipated new people in the monastery, they had to consider what to tell them about contemplative prayer in a new age. In April 1999, three sisters attended a workshop in Ferdinand, Indiana, that was geared toward a proactive approach to vocations. An aggressive strategy aimed at attracting new members and new people involved self-study, a clear sense of mission, and publicity. Eventually, in the context of community discussion and reflection, all the sisters voted to make a five-year commitment to vocations: they were willing to put their primary energy into the steps they believed necessary to recruit new members. Their continuance was connected partly to their own internal process, but also to their ability to draw upon the help and insight of the laity. They needed, for example, to know how they were perceived outside the monastery, and they needed to find ways to make themselves known in a wider arena.

IMAGE COMPLIMENTS OF YOUNG & LARAMORE ADVERTISING

THE WEB SITE

In order to be as effective as possible as they moved forward, the sisters hired Linda Hegeman in January 2000 as director of communications and development. She worked with the sisters to set up a series of focus groups (to provide some information about their visibility in the community), to gather an advisory board, and to make the monastery better known to a broader constituency. After a few months, Ms. Hegeman consulted Young and Laramore, a local advertising agency known for its creative and energetic approaches to difficult issues. The relationship between these hip young advertisers and this group of old cloistered nuns has been one of mutual admiration. When Young and Laramore studied the problem—that the sisters were virtually invisible in the Indianapolis community—they suggested that a Web site might be the best way for the monastery to address issues of visibility and vocation. After several months of design and refinement—each step of which was shared with the sisters—the site was officially launched on March 17, 2001. www.praythenews.com contains some history, explains various aspects of the lives of the sisters, links users with the books for sale in their publishing business, and gives users a way to request prayers. The most unusual feature of the site is its link with contemporary news stories. Each week some of the sisters reflect prayerfully on a pressing news story and share those meditations with the public.

For the last forty years, the sisters have moved steadily toward a new understanding of the ways in which their contemplative life can be more visible and available to the needs of the world. Their emphasis now is to be a contemplative presence to the public in ways that still allow them to maintain their traditional core values of prayer, silence, solitude, and com-

A SUNDAY LITURGY

munity. They are more visible and available today than they once were, no longer separated from people during liturgy, open to meeting with groups to talk about prayer, available for spiritual direction. They believe that they are now being called in new ways to share the contemplative dimension of their lives with those who feel themselves called to a spiritual life. The monastery is a symbol of spiritual adventure, a sign that the world is a holy place, that people are sacred, and that God is present in human lives longing for relationship.

CONCLUDING WITH THE RESURRECTION

The official name of the Indianapolis monastery is the Carmel of the Resurrection, celebrated artistically in the peacock gates that adorn each entrance, and observed each year at Easter. Let me attempt to gather the themes of this book together in an imaginative celebration of the Easter vigil. The removal of the old altar and the installation of the new doors made a statement consistent with changes the sisters had been experiencing over the past two decades. In addition, the flexibility of the space opened new possibilities for liturgy. I can see an Easter vigil consistent with the new doors and their evocation of creation-centered spirituality, a liturgical event rooted in tradition even as it reaches toward new expressions. Typically during this feast, people gather in the lower chapel for the first part and then move up to the choir for the celebration of the Eucharist. Imagine people gathered in the lower chapel in darkness. The new doors are open, and the choir,

GOING TO MASS ON A RAINY DAY

too, is drenched in darkness. Traditionally, in years past people heard stories from the Bible and related them to the elements of fire and water. Tonight there is a sense of fire, water, earth, and air in a swirl of continuous creation, drawing believers deeper into the Mystery of the universe.

Fire: The spirit of God hovers above the chaos. Fifteen billion years ago, the transcendent erupted into being in every moment and every place in the universe. We celebrate that creative emergence in the "Big Bang" and the resplendent formation of the galaxies. "Let there be light," says the Bible story, and the Easter fire is lit.

Water: The creative God is involved in human liberation, first with Noah and then with Moses as the people were led through the parted waters of the Red Sea. Five or six billion years ago, our solar system emerged, and with it our earth. The first inklings of life came in the watery depths of the sea as the warmth of the sun touched it. "If we were baptized into Christ's death, we are baptized into new life," says the New Testament. The baptismal waters are blessed.

Earth: God directs people's lives on earth by way of the Law and the prophets calling people to a new awareness of justice and holiness. Four or five million years ago, hominids emerged from the creative process, eventually becoming what we know today as human beings, populating the earth, traveling everywhere, finding particular expressions of divine life in a myriad of places. "In the end times there will be a new heaven and a new earth," the Bible says. For now we turn to the earth, aware that it contains the hidden God.

Air: The word for air is the same as for breath and for Spirit. God eventually poured out the Holy Spirit on all humankind. Some 40,000 years ago, cultures arose in which, from ancient times to the present, humanity has sought a whole spiritual vision. A God sometimes hidden in darkness has been revealed, and all are called to holiness. Faith is situated in history where God is present, and where contemplatives turn outward to gaze at the wonders of creation and the pain of the world. Faith is also a mystery, deeper in us than breath, calling contemplatives to turn inward, to go deeper into the reality of God as ultimate mystery.

This book has been a celebration of a place and the people who inhabit it, women whose lives have been shaped by fidelity to tradition even as customs have changed and as the world has demanded more engagement from those whose vocations originally inspired them to "leave the world." The story that has unfolded in the lives of these sisters has been complex in some ways and simple in others. The community's belief that the world itself is a sacred space—the result of many years of prayerful discussion, reading, and innovative thinking—is the complicated story I have tried to tell here. The simple part is more mysterious. Letting oneself be drawn into darkness in order to be found by God is, finally, impossible to explain, because it is a risk of the heart. Only by leaping into the depths of that ultimate mystery do the sisters find incomparable sources of life and energy.

Notes

1 Dionysius the Areopagite, sometimes called "Pseudo-Dionysius" or Dionysius the Pseudo-Areopagite, was probably a fifth-century Syrian monk whose spirituality was grounded in neo-Platonism. His writings, especially *The Celestial Hierarchy*, *Mystical Theology*, and *The Divine Names*, are classic expressions of a deeply apophatic spiritual theology that would later inspire such Western mystical classics as *The Cloud of Unknowing* (fourteenth-century England) and the writings of Meister Eckhart (fourteenth-century Rhineland). See *Pseudo-Dionysius: The Complete Works* (New York: Paulist Press, 1987). For a contemporary interpretation of the apophatic tradition, see Denys Turner, *The Darkness of God: Negativity in Christian Mysticism* (Cambridge: Cambridge University Press, 1995).

2 Augustine completed the *City of God* in 476, after nearly fourteen years of reflection and writing. I use the translation of Gerald G. Walsh et al. (New York: Doubleday Image, 1958), p. 467 (Book 19, chapter 19).

3 Bernard of Clairvaux, *Selected Works* (New York: Paulist Press, 1987). In his introduction, Ewert H. Cousins says, "It can be said that for Bernard everything begins and ends with experience, and in between, experience is the object of reflection on God" (p. 31).

4 Julian of Norwich, *Revelations of Divine Love*, translated and with an introduction by Elisabeth Spearing and A. C. Spearing (London: Penguin Books, 1998), p. 38.

5 Jerome Nadal (1507-80), an artist, early Jesuit, and close friend of Ignatius, used this phrase about him. Thanks again to Keith J. Egan for sharing his knowledge of historical tidbits with me.

6 *Writings in Time of War* (London: Collins, 1968), p. 130.

7 See Richard McBrien, "Christian Spirituality," chapter XXVIII in *Catholicism*, vol. II (Minneapolis: Winston Press, 1980), p. 1073.

8 Ursula King, *Spirit of Fire: The Life and Vision of Teilhard de Chardin* (Maryknoll, N.Y.: Orbis Books, 1966), p. 113. This book is one of the best introductions to Teilhard's work and to his life.

9 *Le Milieu Divin: An Essay on the Interior Life* (London: Collins, 1963), p. 136.

10 Walter M. Abbott, ed., *The Documents of Vatican II* (New York: Guild Press, 1966), pp. 65-72.

11 *Cosmology and Creation: The Spiritual Significance of Contemporary Cosmology* (New York: Oxford University Press, 1999), p. 136.

12 *The Universe Story* (New York: Harper and Row, 1992), p. 74.

13 "Romances sobre el Evangelico," in *The Collected Works of St. John of the Cross*, edited by Kieran Kavanaugh and Otilio Rodriguez (Washington, D.C.: Institute of Carmelite Studies Publications, 1979), pp. 724-32.

14 The grille that stood behind that door, and served to separate the community from the public when the doors were open, had been removed in 1969, as noted in the previous chapter.

15 Famously, in the *Life*, chapters 11-22, Teresa explained various stages of prayer by way of water imagery: wells, water wheels, streams, and rain all stand for different kinds of prayer and stages of meditation.

16 Memo from vonRoenn describing the doors (March 1988) from the archives.

CARMEL

Throughout this volume I have used the translations of Kieran Kavanaugh and Otilio Rodriguez for the works of *Teresa of Avila and John of the Cross*. *The Collected Works of Teresa of Avila* is a three-volume set published by the Institute for Carmelite Studies in Washington, D.C. Volume One (revised 1987) contains her *Life* plus "The Spiritual Testimonies" and the "Soliloquies." Volume Two (1980) contains *The Way of Perfection*, "Meditations on the Song of Songs," and *The Interior Castle*. Volume Three (1985) contains *The Book of Her Foundations* along with minor works, including poetry and constitutions. *The Collected Works of St. John of the Cross* are in one volume, published by ICS in 1979.

Because certain terms and usage may not be familiar to some readers, I provide here a short glossary.

CARMEL is a general term that can be used as shorthand for the life within a Carmelite monastery, for the monastery itself, or for Carmelite spirituality in general.

•

CHAPTER usually means a weekly meeting of the sisters who have taken final vows, which includes an inspirational talk by the prioress and discussion of important matters, and ends with mutual sisterly correction. In traditional monastic language, the acknowledgment of transgressions against the rule was called the "chapter of faults." A "general chapter" is a meeting of friars or nuns representing all monasteries within the order.

•

CHARISM comes from the Greek word meaning "gift," and usually means a special gift or calling. It can also be used to signify the spirit of the organization. There is, for example, a Carmelite charism.

•

DISCALCED literally means "without shoes" and is the word that was used to distinguish the reformed communities of Teresa of Avila from other Carmelite communities. A Carmelite with the initials O.C.D. after her name is a member of the Order of Carmelites Discalced.

•

DIVINE OFFICE or Office is sometimes called the "Opus Dei" (the work of God) and is the form of prayer that is said in monastic communities. Traditionally

PREVIOUS SPREAD: MONASTERY FROM S. COLDSPRING ROAD, C. 1936

monks and nuns began the day with Lauds (praising God for a new day) and punctuated the day with the "Little Hours": Prime (directly after morning prayer), Terce (at nine in the morning, the "third hour" of the ancient world), Sext (at midday), and None (at three P.M., or the "ninth hour" of the ancient world, the time when Christ died). They said Vespers and Compline in the evening and Matins in the middle of the night. The schedule has changed over the years. The sisters in Indianapolis say Lauds before daily Mass and meet for Noon prayer and Evening prayer.

•

EXTERNALS refers to various ritual movements during prayer or in meeting another sister, or in acknowledging one's faults in chapter. The Carmelite ceremonial contained specific directions for standing, kneeling, sitting, preparing for bed, washing oneself, etc.

•

FOUNDATION is a term for a "daughter house," i.e., a second group of sisters living in another place. Religious orders with celibate members could grow only through vocations, and when a monastery was crowded, some of those sisters moved to another place to begin a new monastery. The Carmelite monastery of Indianapolis "founded" monasteries in Terre Haute and in Reno, Nevada.

•

GRILLE, sometimes called "grate," is a latticed wall of separation between cloistered sisters and the outside world. Grilles separated the choir from the chapel in church. Sisters in the choir could not be seen by the laity in the chapel. Double grilles were installed in each visiting room so that sisters seeing visitors would be separated from them and unable to touch them.

•

MOTHER was the word that sisters traditionally used to address the prioress (elected community leader). When Sister Theresa of the Trinity left Iowa to establish a new foundation in New Albany, Indiana, she therefore became Mother Theresa of the Trinity.

•

RUBRICS are gestures, usually those made by the priest at Mass, but can be applied more generally as well. The name comes from the fact that they were printed in red (Latin *ruber*) in the books used by the priest in saying Mass.

•

Rule means the specifications for the life led by members of a community. Each religious order has its own Rule, the first of which was written in the sixth century by Saint Benedict. The Rule could be applied to every facet of a sister's life.

•

Sacristy is the room in which the priest dresses for Mass, usually behind or near the altar.

•

Turn or turn room is a means of communication between the outside world and the cloister. It is not a door, since the main enclosure door was always locked and opened only to admit, e.g., doctors in emergencies. Neither is it a gate where deliveries are made. Rather, the turn is a revolving shelf where someone from the outside can place a package that the "turn sister" can then bring inside. The "turn room" is the place that contains the turn itself, and also a small door through which sisters could talk to those ringing the "turn bell."

•

Vocation is from the Latin word meaning calling. Although everyone seeks his or her vocation in life, "a vocation" usually meant a calling to religious life, often to a particular community as in "a vocation to Carmel."

c. 1200	Historical origins of the Carmelite Order in Jerusalem
c. 1209	Formula of life (on which later Rule was based) written
c. 1238	Carmelites begin to move to Europe
1247	Carmelite Rule approved by Pope Innocent IV
1298	Pope Boniface VIII requires strict enclosure for all nuns
1430	General meeting at Nantes produces Mitigated Rule
1452	Pope Nicholas V allows women to become Carmelites
1515	Teresa de Cepeda y Ahumada (Saint Teresa of Avila) born
1535	Teresa enters the monastery of the Incarnation in Avila
1542	Juan de Yepes (Saint John of the Cross) born near Avila
1545-63	Council of Trent meets in three sessions (1545-47, 1551-52, 1562-63)
1562	Teresa's reform begins at Saint Joseph's in Avila
1582	Teresa dies at Alba de Tormes
1591	John of the Cross dies at Ubeda
1604	Teresa's reform movement moves to France
1662	Teresa of Avila canonized

1726 John of the Cross canonized

1790 First Carmelite monastery founded in America (Port Tobacco)

1881 Emma Seelbach born in Kentucky

1911 Baltimore Carmel (Port Tobacco) makes foundation in Bettendorf, Iowa

1912 Emma Seelbach enters the Bettendorf Carmel

1913 Emma Seelbach becomes Sister Theresa of the Trinity

1922 Bettendorf Carmel establishes a foundation in New Albany, Indiana, led by Mother Theresa of the Trinity

1926 John of the Cross named a "doctor of the church"

1932 First wing of the Indianapolis Carmel completed

1936 Mother Theresa dies of a heart attack at age 54

1936 Small addition made to south wing of the monastery

1939 First public outdoor novena held on monastery grounds

1941 Living quarters completed

1947 Monastery makes a foundation in Terre Haute, Indiana

1950 Pope Pius XII encourages cloistered sisters to form federations in *Sponsa Christi*

1953 Permanent enclosure wall finished

1954 Carmelites from other monasteries meet in Indianapolis to discuss possible federation

1954 Monastery makes a foundation in Reno, Nevada

1961 Permanent chapel finished

1965 Carmelites from fifty-four monasteries meet in St. Louis

1969 Some sisters participate in founding of Association of Contemplative Sisters in Woodstock, N.Y.

1970 Indianapolis sisters form an association with other Carmelite sisters

1970 Teresa of Avila named a "doctor of the church"

1988 New doors installed between choir and chapel

1990 Carmelite Order in the United States celebrates its 200th anniversary

1997 Thérèse of Lisieux declared a "doctor of the church"

Photo credits

Except as noted below, all the photographs are courtesy of the Sisters of Our Lady of Mount Carmel, Indianapolis, Indiana. The author gratefully acknowledges the following for permission to reproduce their photographs in this book:

Denis Ryan Kelly Jr.
"Peacock Gate at Monastery Entrance," p. 51

Tony Valainis for *The Indianapolis Monthly*
"Sister Mary Rogers, 2001," p. x
"Sisters in Lower Chapel, 2001," pp. 88-89
"Liturgy of the Hours, 2001," p. 97

Young & Laramore Advertising
"The Web Site," p. 99

Frank Espich, for *The Indianapolis Star*
"Going to Mass on a Rainy Day," p. 101

Bass Archives
"Monastery from S. Coldspring Road, c. 1936," pp. 104-105

Book design: Antenna, Indianapolis
Printer: Hilltop Press, Indianapolis

This book was composed in Adobe Caslon and Trade Gothic. It was printed on Cougar Natural 80lb. text with end sheets of French Speckletone 70lb. text.

"The union between the soul and God
is like starlight united with the light of the sun."
—John of the Cross, "Spiritual Canticle" 26.5